WITHDRAWN

WITHDRAWN

Creating
the
Ethical School

Creating
the
Ethical School

A BOOK OF CASE STUDIES

Bongsoon Zubay
Jonas F. Soltis

FOREWORD BY
ROBERT J. NASH

Teachers College
Columbia University
New York and London

Published by Teachers College Press, 1234 Amsterdam Avenue, New York, NY 10027

Library of Congress Cataloging-in-Publication Data

Zubay, Bongsoon.
  Creating the ethical school : a book of case studies / Bongsoon Zubay, Jonas F. Soltis : foreword by Robert J. Nash.
      p. cm.
  Includes bibliographical references.
  ISBN 0-8077-4514-6 (cloth : alk. paper) — ISBN 0-8077-4513-8 (paper : alk. paper)
    1. Moral education—United States—Case studies. 2. Education—Moral and ethical aspects—United States—Case studies. 3. School improvement programs—United States—Case studies. I. Soltis, Jonas F. II. Title.

LC311.Z83 2004
370.11′4—dc22

                                                                          2004048989

ISBN 0–8077–4513–8 (paper)
ISBN 0–8077–4514–6 (cloth)

Printed on acid-free paper

Manufactured in the United States of America

12 11 10 09 08 07 06 05   8 7 6 5 4 3 2 1

*For my husband, Geoff Zubay, and our son, Geoffrey,
both of whom inspire me with their passion for work
and their dedication to personal and professional ethics.*
—BZ

*To my loving wife, Nancy, who has persevered as my
helpmate in spite of ever-increasing vision loss through
all my books, including this last one.*
—JS

Contents

Preface and Acknowledgments

The idea for and content of this book arose out of a three-year co-curricular theme focused on "Ethics" at the Berkeley Carroll School in Brooklyn, New York, where co-author Bongsoon Zubay was Head for over 25 years. Much effort went into undertaking the project to raise the level of ethical awareness at the school, and during the course of the project much learning took place both individually and collectively about the value of developing a common code of ethics across religious, ethnic, and cultural boundaries in a nonsectarian school environment. So much so, in fact, that it seemed worthwhile to share the lessons learned with teachers and administrators of other schools, both private and public.

The bulk of the book contains ethical cases, and is designed to allow teachers and administrators to select, read, and discuss pertinent cases with one another and with their students, thereby initiating dialogues and discussions about real dilemmas they may encounter in the course of daily school life. It is our hope that this will encourage the discussion of ethical issues as a regular part of the social interaction of any school. We have found that participating in such experiences raises the level of ethical awareness in many positive ways.

The majority of the ethical cases included in this book were written in a workshop for teachers and administrators conducted by co-author Jonas Soltis. Some cases came from other schools and some from Berkeley Carroll, but each is a true story. While each case is presented in the individual writer's style, the names of the characters and places contained within are pseudonyms. The ethical cases and statements of "Student Understandings of Right and Wrong" are presented anonymously, with the names of all contributors listed alphabetically following these acknowledgments.

We are grateful to the board of Trustees at the Berkeley Carroll School for understanding the merit of this book and the universality of these cases and allowing us to use the school's name in connection with them. We are grateful to all of the teachers and administrators at the school, both past and present, who enthusiastically allowed us to include their stories. Each of these educators dedicated much time and effort to working courageously through some very sensitive issues, and in the end were able to help one another and the students learn from their experiences.

We thank the Berkeley Carroll students who were fully engaged in the project and the other independent school educators who took the time to submit ethical cases for this book in the midst of their hectic lives. We are also pleased to acknowledge the members of the Visual Arts Department, Chair Bob Weiss, Susan Haber, Judith Barrett, and the Lower School classroom teachers, for their contribution of student artwork. The artwork shown at the beginning of each chapter was taken from the school's Art Calendar from one of the years when the school focused on "Ethics" as a co-curricular theme.

The final result of our three-year ethical study is a set of "Ethical Standards" written by and for each of the Berkeley Carroll School's constituencies: students, parents, faculty, and administrators. These appear in Appendix B at the end of the book. It is our hope that this book will help each reader develop his or her own tangible set of ethical standards, and that eventually we will all come to realize the importance of practicing ethical behavior in our daily lives.

We want to express our deep gratitude to Assistant to the Head, Cynthia Galko, who conducted oral interviews with faculty members at the end of the three-year Ethics theme to get their feedback on the results of our efforts, and to longtime Administrative Assistant to the Head, Rose Ann Fusillo, for her extensive behind-the-scenes work. Both Cynthia and Rose Ann worked on this manuscript right up until their last day of employment with the Berkeley Carroll School. We also want to thank the Klingenstein Foundation and Professor Pearl Kane of Teachers College, Columbia University for providing the opportunity for our paths to cross in 1994.

Finally, we are most grateful to editor Brian Ellerbeck, who saw the merit of this book, gave us invaluable advice about shaping it into a cohesive form, and helped us make it available to teachers and administrators everywhere.

Foreword

Finally, here is an ethics textbook for educators that is truly a "real world" experience. Jonas Soltis is one of the most well-known applied ethics educators and philosophers of education in the United States. Bongsoon Zubay is less well known, but, in this volume, she proves herself a worthy coauthor and a discerning, passionate applied ethicist. *Creating the Ethical School: A Book of Case Studies* is one of the best ethics primers for teachers and administrators that I have ever read; and I, for one, intend to use it with enthusiasm in my own university ethics courses. I have already highly recommended this text to certain colleagues throughout the country.

What makes this book so special is that it was shaped in the school trenches, emerging from a three-year, co-curricular ethics project at the Berkeley Caroll School in Brooklyn, New York. Zubay was head of the Berkeley Carroll School for over 25 years. She knows students and teachers well from preschool through high school. All of the cases in this book cover an exciting array of ethical dilemmas and issues featuring every grade level. Readers will find in the dozens of ethics cases a cornucopia of real-world moral issues facing teachers, students, administrators, parents, principals, and trustees everywhere.

What I find particularly impressive about this book, in addition to its many wonderfully engaging and challenging ethical case studies, is the underlying philosophy of moral education that punctuates every page. Here is how the authors themselves express it: "The basic premise of this book is that there is an inherent moral and ethical relationship between those who teach and those who are taught. Indeed, teaching the young has a moral dimension because education itself is a moral endeavor. . . . The place we call school is an environment of moral interaction and sometimes moral struggle." This assertion, in my opinion, is succinct, cogent, and dead-on, and it has been confirmed time and time again in my own extensive work with educators at all levels of schooling, including college.

Here is a veteran administrator, Zubay, in an urban K–12, independent school, asserting: "[T]he teaching and learning of ethical awareness in the intellectual and social learning environment of a school is as critical as the three R's and the acquisition of knowledge in any academic discipline." And also: "I became more and more convinced that ethical awareness, ethical reasoning, and ethical behavior needed to become part of the fabric of our school's life." In my own experience in teaching hundreds of courses geared to educational leaders, these assertions are truly revolutionary. Zubay's moral vision for both independent and public schools, enhanced by her longstanding work on ethics and educational philosophy with Soltis, a Columbia University Teachers College Professor, is striking.

The first chapter unfolds as a clear and forceful narrative explaining in detail how Zubay and Soltis got involved in constructing, and implementing, the three year co-curricular ethics theme for the Berkeley Carroll School. The rest of the chapters feature several true ethics case-dilemmas, which occurred in a variety of preschool, middle-school, and high school settings. Each of the cases is written in a realistic, provocative, and ethically challenging manner. They can be adapted to either private or public school settings.

Consider are a few examples of some of the more enticing titles of the ethical dilemmas. "The Case of the Taunted Loner." "Racism? Or Just Teasing?" "A Violent Cheater." "To Copy or Not To Copy?" "But Is It Plagiarism?" "Cultural Identity." "A Rumored Affair." "Anorexia and Responsibility." "The School as Parent." "Student Newspaper: Free Speech and Administrative Responsibility."

Furthermore, the authors design each case in such a way that educators and students at all levels can experience firsthand the complexities of ethical inquiry and decision-making. Writing an applied ethics text is no small task for most ivory tower ethicists-authors to perform; yet Zubay and Soltis are willing and able to leave the rarified atmosphere of moral philosophy and ethical theory, disciplines they know well, in order to speak directly to those professionals and students who live and work every day in the educational trenches.

What will readers of this book learn about how to raise ethical awareness in schools? They will gain a clearer understanding of the ethical principles that underlie their schools' rules and policies. They will learn how to create a moral ethos in their schools, an ethos that is civil, just, pluralistic, and nurturing. They will learn how to defend ethical decision-making, as well as how to stimulate probing ethical inquiry.

They will become sensitive to the multiple moral perspectives characteristic of all constituencies in any educational venture. They will understand, however, that despite the diversity of moral points of view present in educational organizations, consensual ethical decision-making is desirable, possible, and, indeed, achievable in the nation's schools.

Equally important, and innovative, in my view, are the book's two appendices. Appendix A presents a developmental view of how students from preschool to high school process and articulate what's "right and wrong." This developmental moral view has been long-needed for ethics educators in the schools. The many examples of students' moral comments in Appendix A are genuinely enlightening. And Appendix B presents specific "ethical standards" drawn up by each of the constituencies of the Berkeley Carroll School. In my opinion, these standards are universalizable for all levels of schooling everywhere.

I hope that readers take the time to examine these appendices carefully. They provide the background necessary for educators to enhance the ethical awareness of their school communities. In fact, I hope that readers examine the entire book carefully. Its potential moral impact on schools throughout the country could very well be transformative.

—ROBERT J. NASH

Illustration by Caitlin Cahill, Brian McGillin, Brian Oppenheim, &
Erica Stone, Kindergarteners (a cooperative project)

1

Nurturing Ethical Consciousness in a School Community

Cultivate Virtue in yourself,
And Virtue will be real.
Cultivate it in the family
And Virtue will abound.
Cultivate it in the village,
And virtue will grow.
Cultivate it in the nation,
And Virtue will be abundant.
Cultivate it in the universe,
And Virtue will be everywhere.
—LAO-TZU, CIRCA 500 BC

This book is a collection of ethical dilemma case studies drawn from real-life situations in schools. It was compiled and edited by a school head and a philosopher of education who worked together for three years trying to develop a pedagogy of ethics in an urban pre-K–12, nonsecular, independent school. Its purpose is to provide any school or school system, public or private, with a vehicle for raising the ethical consciousness of its teachers, students, administrators, parents, and staff. This can be done by discussing these case studies among different constituent school groups in classrooms, meetings, workshops, seminars, retreats, assemblies, and other school-sponsored events. We have found that having serious moral conversations about real ethical dilemmas in school settings generates a very high level of communal awareness of the pervasiveness and need for ethical considerations in schools.

This book also can be used to underwrite the teaching and learning of ethics as an integral part of the curriculum, which we set out to do at the Berkeley Carroll School. Used this way, its goal is to empower educators, private and public, to teach ethics, age-appropriately, as an embedded part of their curriculum and in the context of their school as a social environment and an agent for positive change. As with any educational initiative, we knew that the teacher had to be at the heart of an ethics curriculum's effective implementation. We found that using case studies told by teachers themselves encouraged discussion and sharing of ethical concerns and values among the teachers and made them more comfortable as they sought to infuse their classrooms with ethical awareness and moral conversation. Other case studies in this book—by students, parents, administrators, and heads of schools—provide insight into ways in which diverse school communities using a case studies approach can come together to find common ground, mobilize for action, and raise ethical awareness among all their constituencies.

This is not, however, a formal or academic ethics text. Survey courses and basic texts on ethics are readily available to those who wish to gain a more abstract understanding of classical and modern ethical theories. For those interested in more formal work, we have added a short list of suggested readings at the end of this book. We did find, however, that as our realistic cases were discussed, people quite naturally referred to basic ethical principles to justify their decisions, and they intuitively approached ethical decision-making using one of two theoretically relevant basic strategies.

Theoretically, all ethical decision-making can be generally categorized as either consequentialist or nonconsequentialist. When people call upon an ethical principle or rule such as the principle of "honesty" or the rule "always tell the truth" to justify a proposed solution to an ethical dilemma, they are among those in the nonconsequentialist camp, who basically say, "One must do the right thing no matter what." If, however, people consider the possible consequences of a proposed action and judge the rightness of the act by the goodness or fairness of the state of affairs that comes after the decision/action, then they have come down in the theory camp of the consequentialists who say, like the Hippocratic Oath, "do no harm." So perhaps if one lies about the ethnic identity of a neighbor to a group of genocidal murderers, the consequences of lying in this case would be better than the consequences of telling the truth.

We all bring to our daily dealings with others implicit ethical principles and consequentialist and/or nonconsequentialist approaches to our moral decision-making. Just as we can speak English before or even without taking an English course, we can and do seriously discuss and make reasonable and justifiable ethical decisions. This does not mean that the formal study of ethics is unnecessary or to be avoided. To the contrary, we encourage and invite our readers to use our suggested readings in moral theory to help them to begin to formulate their own ethical positions more articulately and more abstractly. In fact, the prompting questions we have added to the end of each case study were designed to help readers focus on the ethical principles and alternate approaches possibly relevant to the case so they could articulate, examine, and discuss them. Thus, we aim at creating an atmosphere for serious moral conversations to take place that will emphasize good reasons and rational thinking as well as empathy and open-mindedness.

This, then, is a book primarily for those who want to raise their awareness of the pervasiveness of real ethical situations that arise in the school context and also have an opportunity to think deeply and ethically about them in dialogue with other members of the school community. We have found that case study discussions with others provide a wonderful opportunity for each participant to dig underneath his or her knee-jerk reactions or thoughtless rule followings to examine and apply the ethical principles we more often than not hold in common as members of the same community; to listen to the reasons and ideas of others that may help us to see other ethical dimensions in the case that we were blind to; and to reach a sense of communal commitment to the thoughtful solution of moral dilemmas in one's school and to the building of an ethical educational community.

THE MORAL NATURE OF EDUCATION

The basic premise of this book is that there is an inherent moral and ethical relationship between those who teach and those who are taught. Indeed, teaching the young has a moral dimension because education itself is a moral endeavor. It is concerned with the development of human beings and human interactions. Whenever a teacher asks a student to share something with another student, decides between two students in a schoolyard dispute, discusses the welfare of a student with another teacher, or handles plagiarism and dishonesty, moral considerations are present.

There is a moral component in classroom instruction as well. The moment the door closes and class begins, teachers have to make choices that affect the present and future development of their students as persons. One choice might be to slow down the pace of instruction to accommodate the needs of those students who require extra time, or to move the class forward for the majority who are tuned into the instructional materials presented, perhaps leaving others behind and less prepared for their futures. Another choice might be to punish or not punish the whole class for being very noisy even though some students weren't noisy at all.

The place we call school is an environment of moral interaction and sometimes moral struggle. Children's ability to expand moral sensitivity and ethical reasoning skills will very much depend upon how adults around them model ethical behavior and ethical reasoning. Essentially, a teacher's conduct, at all times and in all ways, is a moral matter. The level of collegial actions between teachers as well as the negative or positive comments one teacher makes about another in formal or informal situations also has an impact on how students perceive the modeling of professionalism and moral sensitivity in adults. How teachers and administrators treat students, justly or unjustly, tolerantly or intolerantly, compassionately or mechanically, all model a moral perspective toward others.

Similarly, parenting is a moral endeavor. What parents say about their children's school and its teachers has a direct impact on the way their children perceive their school and their teachers, and whether or not they learn respect and trust in their school environment. How parents handle their children's misbehavior or cruelty to peers also is mirrored in their children's ethical behaviors. How parents act in their own moral situations models for their children the ethical life.

Today's children have to deal with much more than teachers and parental influences on their ethical lives and values, however. Society and popular culture have an enormous impact. Not only are our streets unsafe and violence an everyday occurrence, but holders of public office are charged with serious breaches of ethics, young people abuse drugs and vandalize, television and the movies celebrate violence and sex, and even ordinary courtesy and civility are hard to find in our public spaces. Students see vast differences between what adults preach and what they practice. Rather than being concerned with what's right and what's wrong, our children's ethical choices too often devolve in a moral relativism and indifference. Trust, justice, and honesty in our society have eroded to such an extent that there are no unambiguous heroes whom our children can look up to.

At the center of this ethical chaos, we find teachers and parents who are in the company of children for many of their waking hours, but who may, in fact, have vastly different expectations for these same children. The lives of school teachers and administrators would be simplified if the fit between the expectations of the parents and those of the school were better. Schools and the people in them are caught up in a host of contradictions and the inevitable conflicts between individual and group interests. One would hope that teachers and administrators would be well prepared to deal with these contradictions and conflicts in fulfilling their educational mission. Unfortunately, this is not always an easy task. When we talk about political or moral correctness, the term "correctness" sounds more like what is outwardly convenient than what is morally correct. Caught in a morass of fuzzy relativism and indecision about the place of ethics in school, teachers, administrators, and parents fear prescribing what "should" be done. This is precisely why we need an open dialogue with parents, administrators, and teachers in search of common values to use when teaching ethics to our students.

But a school bent on the ethical education of the young needs more than this. It needs to find ways to engage the whole school in ethical issues, in moral deliberation, and in sensitive, empathetic, and sympathetic exchanges and interactions. To give the reader a flavor of the kind of real-life case studies collected for this volume, we find it appropriate here to let one of the co-authors tell her own story of how this book came about.

THE SCHOOL HEAD'S STORY

When I first became the head of a school in the mid-1970s, it was a banner time for education. There was a firm rejection of the "one size fits all" educational philosophy of the past, and researchers were engaged in a variety of experiments designed to make the teaching and learning environment more responsive to the needs of the individual student. Idealistic baby boomers were having their first children, determined to raise them far differently from their parents; they wanted to be directly involved in their children's schooling and to have ownership in the process. Many parents got together and founded their own schools that represented an eclectic blend of the best ideas and philosophies of the time.

One such school hired me as their headmistress in 1976. Founded as a Montessori school by a group of parents, the school was located in a gentrified and newly landmarked New York City neighborhood. Enrollment at all levels was rapidly expanding, and parents were desperate for the school to expand through the middle-school years so that there would be a continuum in their children's educations.

Change, growth, and risk-taking were already part of this small ten-year-old school. Having made a career transition from classroom teacher to one of the youngest heads in the New York City independent school community, I had no choice but to be fearless in this new and daunting role. Fortunately, I also was incredibly idealistic. I thought of the opportunity to lead this school as a gift—I envisioned my new school as an intellectual haven where highly motivated and bright children were taught by equally motivated and bright teachers. I wanted to reach out to the school's energetic and well-informed parent body and make them an essential part of our learning community. I was committed to recruiting and retaining outstanding teachers who would embrace the school's mission, enjoy the company of children, and grow professionally on the job. With a visionary and committed board of trustees and a strong parent partnership, the school prospered.

In these early years, I believed that intellect, commitment to a given task, and creativity were the three critical components that teachers ought to bring out and elicit from every child. It was the teacher's responsibility to motivate the student to learn, to help children stay with a given task even when difficult, and to teach problem-solving and critical thinking skills. At our school, teachers had real ownership for the children in their care and were expected to know how each child learned differently. They were trained to offer accelerated programs to high-achieving students and extra help and attention to the children who were struggling on their road to academic success.

For a large number of children, the schooling process is not easy. So much depends on verbal skills and one's competency in writing and reading that students whose skills are not in the top range often struggle not only with their schoolwork but with their self-esteem. When Howard Gardner published his first book on multiple intelligences, *Frames of Mind: Multiple Intelligence Theory*, in 1983, I was so happy for those students whose strengths did not rest in verbal and logical-mathematical skills. As a head of school, I was thrilled that I no longer needed to emphasize excellence in verbal and quantitative skills as the only paths to school success. Gardner's seven types of intelligence—verbal ability, logical-mathematical reasoning skills, spatial ability, musical ability, body-kinesthetic ability, interpersonal skills, and intrapersonal skills—gave me a basis on which to promote our school's mission of bringing out "excellence in every child" in a broader context.

By this time in our school's development, I was heading a two-campus, comprehensive, pre-kindergarten through 12th-grade college preparatory school with a heterogeneous and coed population. Classroom teachers and administrators on all grade levels could apply Gardner's multiple intelligences theory in their pedagogy, and they were encouraged to do so. At every meeting for teachers, for students, and for parents, I talked about bringing out excellence in every child and how one's interpersonal and intrapersonal skills were integral to the student's success in school and later the workplace. I explained that every school had students whose strengths were varied in the seven intelligences, and that our school's job was to identify and promote the particular strengths that each child brings to the school, to work on building strength upon strength, to address weaknesses, and to generate strong self-esteem in every child.

We as a school community emphasized the development of interpersonal and intrapersonal intelligences. We made it clear that every student was expected to be a responsible individual and to accept responsibility for one's actions, to extend oneself above and beyond one's own success in school, to reach out to others, to understand others' needs, to learn to develop empathy, and to be kind.

Did this mean that our school was immune from children's usual developmental manifestations of social cruelty, cheating, teasing, stealing, and bullying? Absolutely not. In fact, these were issues with which I regularly dealt in my tenure as head of school.

Manifestation of cruelty is often hidden from adults in school, and in my experience children always know exactly when, where, and how they can exercise ruthless cruelty and flex their muscles to test their social place with certain peer groups. In the case of very young children, a teacher's stern reproach, reasoning, and talking about consequences usually works as a check on their negative behavior. As children reach middle-school age, however, they become rather feisty and skillful in articulating why and how certain actions or events took place. They effortlessly blame others while making themselves look like innocent bystanders. In high school, students work very hard to establish their autonomy and independence in the world of adults and, in so doing, are cynical. They test limits and have a strong desire to deviate from school rules and policies. Their assertion of who they are and what they want to become is often not in sync with their parents' thinking or values. Peer pressure complicates matters: no high school student ever wants to report on the plagiarism, stealing, or substance abuse of one's peers. It seems to take real courage to notify an adult about a peer behaving in a self-destructive mode.

The social dynamics required to deal with these ethical situations have become more and more a part of the educational process, often with the teacher in the role of a referee and the administrator in the role of judge and jury. At our school, the outcomes of these interactions were almost always unsatisfying and frustrating. When teachers would talk to the parents of both the culprit and the victim of social cruelty, for example, the parents would often blame the behavior on a lack of teacher supervision or on the other child. Parents couldn't understand that the child seen in the school environment could be very different from the child seen at home as a son, daughter, and sibling. In response to a lack of dialogue and understanding from parents, our teachers felt disrespected and unappreciated. They didn't want to be accused of wrongdoing in disciplinary measures, and so they either ignored the problem or they referred cases to the school psychologist or the chief administrator of the division.

As our enrollment grew—and as our society changed, with an ever-increasing emphasis on power, success, and personal ambition—so, too, did these ethical cases. It wasn't long before I realized that the teaching and learning of ethical awareness in the intellectual and social learning environment of school is as critical as the three R's and the acquisition of knowledge in any academic discipline. Most important, I saw that ethical awareness has to be taught and learned by the examples one sees and observes in the actions of teachers and administrators in school.

I was in a quandary. How could we begin to delve into moral issues without talking about morality directly? Where would we begin? With teachers? With parents? With students? Who could initiate such a dialogue without offending others? If we didn't want to offend anyone, could we shift the focus to a benign effort aimed at instilling a strong sense of community among all our constituents? How would that approach work?

As I thought through these questions, I recalled my own experience as a parent who was in awe of my child and his development from infancy onward. Just as everyone is born with human intelligence, so, too, do I believe that every child is born with a certain moral fiber. An infant, so dependent on the primary caregiver, learns when to trust and when not to trust depending on how his needs are met. Through trial and error, an infant reacts to the relationship. It is from child rearing at home and human interactions in the social milieu of the school environment that children continue to develop their morality. They get the sense of what's right and wrong, what's appropriate behavior and what isn't, how not to hurt others, and how to protect themselves. The ways in which adults nurture, encourage, and challenge the fundamental morality in children during their developmental stages into adulthood has a profound impact in instilling unconscious moral behaviors and actions.

Next, I thought of our teachers and the range of moral judgments and ethical behaviors I had observed in their human interactions in the school setting. Some teachers were superb in their subject matter but had shallow ethics in their dealings with children as well as the adults with and for whom they worked. Others were so self-righteous and morally superior that they refused to have a dialogue with anyone who disagreed with their viewpoint. Many found it difficult to admit making a mistake or an error in judgment with their students, or with their colleagues. Then there were teachers who clearly expressed the notion that they were teachers of their subject and that alone; they would close their eyes to unacceptable behaviors and language spoken among some children. It was not their role to intervene; discipline was someone else's job.

I became more and more convinced that ethical awareness, ethical reasoning, and ethical behavior needed to become part of the fabric of our school's life. What I needed was a mechanism to implement this goal. I found that in our school's annual co-curricular theme. The idea of a co-curricular theme came about as a means of promoting unity and a strong sense of community and purpose in our diverse school, a school that ranged from pre-kindergarten through 12th grade at two different locations. In its first year, the theme was science and mathematics; among the other themes were performing arts, humanities, leadership, gender studies, creativity, community service, and the environment. For every theme, the school administration and Parent Association would sponsor lectures by one or two prominent speakers every year; for gender studies, we had Myra and David Sadker of American University; for science and mathematics, John Allen Paulos, professor and author of *Innumeracy*.

In early 1994, I had the good fortune of learning about the ethics of teaching from Professor Jonas Soltis of Teachers College, Columbia University. Professor Soltis was on the faculty of the Klingenstein Visiting Heads program, a monthlong fellowship of intensive study for ten heads of independent schools from across the country. It was here that I discovered a mentor in Professor Soltis and a potential partner for implementing an ethical awareness program at my school. I knew then that no school administrator could undertake a program of this magnitude alone; we needed an outside expert to guide us.

I laid out my plan to our school's administrators, and after much deliberation ethics was chosen as a co-curricular theme, with a special focus on "searching for common values in educating children."

Administrators felt this was such a weighty topic that it needed two years for implementation.

Presenting the study of ethics as a co-curricular theme to the wider community was not an easy task. Faculty and administrators were skeptical of raising ethical issues in our school, where enormous diversity in religion, race, and ethnicity were present. Many felt that as a nonsectarian school we should have a hands-off policy in regard to religion or religious traditions. Others saw ethics as another version of political correctness, a topic they disdained. At the same time, there were some parents who questioned, "Why ethics in school? Isn't this the role of parents? Schools should be teaching skills and other related subjects."

To start off the study of ethics, I began with the faculty and laid out a platform. At the first faculty meeting of the school year, I told teachers that our dialogue on ethics should be viewed with the following assumptions:

- We learn our moral principles just as we learn our native language, from our culture.
- We can view ethical reasoning as a skill that is acquired through practice.
- The ethical behaviors students exhibit and the ethical choices students make in the school environment can be taught age-appropriately.
- Parents can make a difference by helping their children internalize moral values—that is, by internalizing the standards of right and wrong, developing empathetic responses to other people's feelings, and constructing personal standards of kindness and fairness.
- Adults in schools both informally and formally make an impact in shaping and influencing our students as we attempt to bring out excellence in every child.
- We can achieve our goal of bringing out the ethics of excellence in our school community if parents and the school work to find common moral values.

Early in November the entire faculty, administrators, and student representatives from the Upper School participated in a full-day workshop with Professor Soltis. All of us did homework before the workshop by reading his book *The Ethics of Teaching.* Most of the first visit was devoted to small-group discussions on ethical deliberations that related to the cases we had read. Student participation was substantial as they voiced their experiences in wrestling with ethical choices in their interactions with teachers and peers.

Subsequent to the first workshop, teachers and the participating students wrote examples of ethical cases based on their experiences in school. As expected, most cases dealt with dilemmas in interactions with colleagues, administrators, students, and parents. Professor Soltis joined us for a second visit in January to read and discuss selected cases in two separate groups.

Administrators and teachers learned a great deal from these sessions. Through reading and discussing cases written by their colleagues or themselves, we saw more than ever how often we face complex ethical issues. Each day we make choices with our colleagues, students, and parents, without having enough time to pause and reflect on their ethical implications. It was good for us to raise the level of awareness in the decision-making process by listening to others.

Teachers also realized how important it is to be aware of how they speak to children about such issues. They talked about the many ways to get the children involved, including celebrating caring and goodness in assemblies. They talked about having more discussions about common values they want to pass on to our students, as well as having an ethical dialogue with students above and beyond the immediate context of the curriculum, even with preschoolers and kindergartners.

Once a dialogue was established with our faculty, we reached out to parents. Once again, Professor Soltis joined the first parent meeting, at which we asked for their commitment to this partnership in search of a common vision on raising ethical standards in our school community. At the meeting, which was well attended, parents were asked to generate a list of the qualities, values, and moral traits that they hoped their children would have as they grow up and become ethical adults. The list was a long one, and agreement was surprisingly universal among all in this pluralistic group. A shared sense of common values and ethical/moral aims permeated the discussion. This set the tone for parental support of our co-curricular theme, ethics.

The next step was giving our students a forum to express what they knew as "right from wrong." At our annual All School Write-In, every student, from pre-K through 12th grade, wrote an essay on how they knew right from wrong and described an incident in which it took courage to do the right thing. Teachers made selections from the varied responses; the authors were asked to read their essays at the All School Write-In Assembly. We include sample selections of their writings in Appendix A at the end of this book.

The two-year study was so intellectually stimulating that our administration voted to have a third year of ethics as a co-curricular theme. Throughout this time, efforts were undertaken to discuss ethical issues and dilemmas across the curriculum, particularly in literature, history, and science classes. High school advising groups discussed current issues and events in which the morality and the ethics of individuals were questioned. In addition, we had the good fortune of having three college presidents as guest speakers at the commencement exercises, each speaking on the topic of ethics.

Leon Botstein, president of Bard College, spoke to our graduates about being an adult after the turn of the century. He described what he called the current "vacuum of belief in our age of skepticism, relativism, and intolerance." He warned that we have lost our ability to use language in the tyranny of cliches of the mass media, and advised our graduates to stand up for their beliefs, to articulate them while listening to others, and to be candid and truthful and to realize the limits of individualism.

Claire Gaudiani, president of Connecticut College, talked to the graduates about the "wisdom tradition" they inherit as educated persons. Drawing from the great texts of the past, she reminded them of our ethical heritage of virtues and ideals, which includes the concepts of justice, generosity, charity, compassion, tolerance, commitment, integrity, and respect. She challenged them to go beyond the attainment of intellectual skills to develop their humane skills and civic virtues and become good world citizens.

Frank Macchiarola, president of St. Francis College, spoke on law and ethics and told our graduates the story of his immigrant father, who "knew that living a lawful life, believing in the rights of others, and giving good counsel so that people who were contemplating bad things would avoid them and instead choose lives of morality and decency, were the right things to do." Dr. Macchiarola made a distinction between those who use the law and those who live by the ethics behind the law. He urged our graduates to believe in principles that will identify their responsibilities to others, and that will define their duty and obligations as well as their character and meaning in life.

We concluded the three-year co-curricular theme by having each constituency of the school—students, faculty, administration, and parents—write their collective ethical standards. In most cases, a small group of leaders from each constituency drafted their respective standards of ethics, which was then presented to their constituency for revision and subsequent approval. These Ethical Standards are reproduced in Appendix B at the end of this book.

We learned much in our three years and are still learning. The next section provides an overview of the numerous topics treated in the case studies we developed and the student age-related responses to our question of how they perceive the difference between right and wrong.

ORGANIZATION OF THE CASE STUDIES CHAPTERS

We have already indicated the central role the discussion of case studies has played in our journey to become an ethical school. Because, in many instances, an independent school presents a unique type of educational environment, we found that we needed our own cases for our own individual and collective experiences to make the business of everyday decision-making real for the participating constituents of our particular school community. We would urge users of this book to do the same thing. If they are public school–based, it should not be difficult to mentally change the persona in most of our cases from *school head* to *principal* or *superintendent*, and to change *school board of trustees* to *board of education members*. Then, after sufficient experience with our cases, writing your own should be easy. Providing a useful resource for others is what the case studies of our book are about. But even though our focus is on the independent school milieu, we believe there is much in these cases that can and does speak to public school educators. Certain moral dilemmas of school are ubiquitous. They appear with predictable regularity in any school setting, public or private, as you will see as you read and use our cases.

There are many possible ways to organize this presentation of our self-produced cases so they can be sampled and selected from for different purposes by anyone wanting to use this rich resource. More often than not, case titles, while not quite literal, do point fairly clearly to the issue or topic dealt with in the case, so an issue-centered organization was contemplated. But it became clear to us that often the personas or context of a case better sorted groups of cases written from different perspectives of teachers, students, parents, staff, and heads. Hence we have grouped our cases in six chapters each reflecting a relationship and/or a conflict between these various school constituents, e.g. Teacher/Student, Teacher/Administrator, Teacher/Parent, and so forth.

Moreover, we came to appreciate that grouping cases in this way provides an opportunity to explore multiple perspectives on moral and ethical dilemmas across the whole school community. Unique to this book also is Appendix A, which provides insight into the ways in which younger to older students try to make sense of the concepts of right and wrong in their own experience. Too often adults forget that children's minds and moral sensibilities develop and mature over time. Trying to create a nurturing ethical environment in a school requires adult sensitivity and understanding of how children and youth think and grow ethically.

Our first case studies chapter, Chapter 2, provides a group of cases located in the central educational relationship between teachers and students. Among the case studies situations treated are: a teacher phones a parent to report a student's misbehavior and subsequently finds that the child was badly beaten because of her call. A student on drugs pleads with her teacher not to report her so she can finish her final exams and graduate. A grateful computer student offers free software to his teacher that is obviously copyrighted. Should he take it? When student cheating is suspected, how much evidence is necessary to warrant punishment? Is punishment the only moral and educational recourse? These and other issues that arise in the nexus of the teacher/student relationship are explored in depth.

Chapter 3 considers cases and ethical issues that arise when teachers and school administrators interact. Reviewing a teacher's narrative evaluation of a student whose family is friendly with the principal, a teacher is asked by the principal to make "editorial" revisions that elevate her assessment. A teacher suspects that one of her students is being sexually abused at home and is hiding the fact. The teacher goes to the school counselor and then to the principal, both of whom say there is insufficient evidence to do anything. What should she do? A teacher and media center head have serious differences about the fair use clause of the copyright law. There is a shortage of books and other educational materials in the school and minimal copying for student seems fair, but is it against the law as, the media head contends?

Chapter 4 deals with issues that arise when parents and teachers see things differently. A parent urges the teacher to give lower grades to her son because she thinks he is lazy and needs to understand that life isn't always going to be kind and easy. The parent argues that a character-building lesson is better than learning little things her son will never use and probably forget. A social studies teacher leads a discussion about the current government military action being undertaken in the Middle East, which many citizens are undecided about. He helps the students draft a letter of opposition to the war and sends it to the President. Many parents are incensed that the teacher has made political pawns of their sons and daughters. A parent always picks up his 1st-grade daughter at the end of school. Sometimes he comes to the classroom and sits down to talk about his daughter; sometimes he berates the teacher; sometimes he just whisks his daughter away, obviously angry; always he smells of alcohol. What should the teacher do?

Teachers are not only co-workers but also professionals. Chapter 5 treats cases that involve conflicts in both roles. There is the case of a new teacher who observes the class of a veteran teacher and is dismayed at the lack of discipline, the yelling at the children, the rewarding of inappropriate behavior, and the lack of learning going on. What to do? A French teacher is pressed by the PE teacher/baseball coach to pass a borderline-failing student who pitches for the team. What to do? A well-respected senior student reluctantly tells his math teacher that a girl in the class is having an affair with another teacher in the math department. What to do?

Chapter 6 looks at conflicts between parents and administrators. A child completes a full year of preschool but still is two months short of the age of acceptance into kindergarten. Moreover, the preschool staff judges that another year of preschool experience would better ready the boy for kindergarten. The parents insist that he be admitted to kindergarten or they will withdraw him from the school. The school head must make a decision. Another school head is informed by the parents of an anorexic girl that she is in therapy. He asks if the parents are also going to the therapist. They are not. The head knows from experience that without family therapy, a long-term cure for anorexia is not very likely. Is this a school problem or a private one? Should the head do anything? The parents of a child who has serious behavior problem in school are called in to discuss the issue with the school head. They both work long hours and do not have the time to discipline the child at home. They insist that it is the responsibility of the school to teach their child discipline and that is what they are paying for. What responsibility does a school have to the parents, to the child, to the provision of a good learning environment in the school?

Chapter 7 deals with the interaction between heads, trustees, and the school as a school. The trustees of a financially beleaguered school with dwindling enrollments in its K–6 program decided to close the program and sell its buildings to help support the remaining upper and middle school. The school head had urged them to keep the elementary program. The board asked the trustee who served on the committee recommending that the school be sold and who was a realtor to handle the sale. When informed about this decision, the school head realized the commission on the property would be quite substantial and that this clearly was a case of conflict of interest. He approached the executive committee of the board and insisted that the sale be placed with a non-school-related realtor or else he would resign as head. The story of how this conflict was resolved is an interesting one. So, too, is the story of a school trying to monitor and control proper conduct on the use of computers and the Internet. It seems that hacker students are not held back by a school honor code, nor are plagiarism or the use of obnoxious language. The head and trustees decide to close down the whole computer system until the guilty students confess, no matter how long that takes. Many however, wonder why the whole school should be punished for the infractions of a few. There are other stories in this chapter about school head tensions with board chairs, school newspaper codes of conduct problems, and heads letting go of long-term employees. The moral quandaries of school life permeate every constituency of the school community.

In Appendix A, we display a sample of the actual answers students of different age groups give to the question of how they understand right and wrong. Given the work of Piaget, Kolberg, Gilligan, et al. on cognitive and moral development in young children, we know theoretically that moral sophistication is achieved over time. This appendix contains a selection of student statements on what constitutes the basis for morality in the minds of young people from pre–K to 12th grade. This will provide some insight into their developing perceptions of the ethical dilemmas. We need to know how students in our schools approach ethical situations and how they can be helped to move toward a more sophisticated understanding of the moral sphere. After all, it is the students we seek most to influence by nurturing them in an ethical environment. We have arranged their statements in age/grade order. Students were asked to respond to this essay question (an oral answer from the young children): How do you know what is right from wrong? Describe a situation where you acted on what you knew was right when it took courage to do so.

For the youngest, the question was, "How do you know when something is right or wrong?" Pre–K and kindergarten answers were often only one sentence, but give a clue to how the youngest think morally. For example, answers included: if someone pinches, it's wrong; someone will say "good boy/good girl"; when you do something that makes people feel better, that's right. When you bite someone it's wrong because you hurt them and they cry. By 4th grade students are saying things like; when you do something right you feel good inside, but if you do something wrong you don't feel as good as you thought you'd feel.

In middle school students say they know what's right and wrong because their parents taught them; their teacher influences their behavior toward being good; or a person gets a funny feeling inside when they do wrong and a good feeling when they do right; one fights a devil on one shoulder and an angel on the other. By 8th grade a few begin to say things like "The truth is, there's no real way to tell right from wrong" and "Knowing right from wrong is a matter of opinion and choosing right from wrong is a matter of choice."

The high school students offer a wide range of answers. For example, "My conscience tells me" or "national and local laws tell me" or "Doing something wrong is doing that which in the long run will harm you or another." Some believe that "most people don't know right from wrong," and others believe "that we just know it because it's part of our human nature to know right from wrong." Many refer to central virtues such as being honest, upright, having courage, having a conscience, having a compassionate heart, and so forth. There is much more in this appendix, and reading it can be an eye-opener to how students at various ages think about the moral sphere. There also are references in the suggested reading list to books by developmental psychologists that go into greater depth describing and theorizing about the moral development of children.

We also include, in Appendix B, the ethical standards statements developed by each unit of our administrators, parents, faculty, and students as our project drew to a close. We hope the users of this book will find that they can enhance their own school's mission to develop educated persons and good citizens by raising their ethical awareness and engaging them in meaningful moral conversations and reflective considerations.

We end our book with a list of Selected Readings on Moral Theory and Ethics and Education for those who would like to probe more deeply into ethics as a formal subject of study.

SHARING IDEAS ABOUT AIMS

There are many things we tried and are still trying to do to make ourselves an ethical school. Users of this book may find this brief list of some of the most important ones helpful as they embark on their own journeys into moral education.

1. Encourage identification of and reflection on the ethical principles that underwrite certain school rules and actual decisions made at the school.
2. Help a diverse, pluralist community come to see those ethical values, moral principles, and virtues that they hold in common as members of the school community.

3. Create an ethical environment, a morally sensitive community that acts with civility, virtue, and justice in the daily business of living together.
4. Create a morally nurturing place for students, a school with many adult exemplars of the virtues of honesty, responsibility, courage, and principled behavior, a place that demonstrates that ethics is not only an individual thing, but also the consideration of the rights of others.

In our use of cases, we have tried to:

1. Help people articulate what moral principles they already hold and see ethical justification as a public process in a school.
2. Help people see other points of view and other possibilities for just solutions to ethical problems. Sometimes the insights of others help us see ethical dilemmas from a better perspective.
3. Help people see that there is no need to be an "absolute relativist" or "moral skeptic" when there is ethical disagreement. Some solutions are better and more just than others.
4. Help people engage genuinely in moral conversations and thereby see that ethics is an important part of everyone's education and that ethical reasoning is a skill that needs to be cultivated.

Illustration by Cristina Melendez-Picon, Grade 2

2

Teacher/Student Cases

At the heart of all educational endeavors is the teacher/student relationship. This is the focal context for the ethical case studies in this chapter. The teacher is generally taken to be in a position of authority over the student(s), and many ethical issues can arise in the use and/or abuse of that authority. The student(s), on the other hand, have obligations and responsibilities as students, and breaches of these often constitute ethical lapses.

In this chapter, teachers and students confront the problems of discipline, parents' rights, child abuse, bullying, punishment, grading, drugs, confidentiality, racism, and cheating. A host of subsidiary contextual problems also arise and force the consideration of basic ethical principles such as fairness, justice, honesty, respect, and evaluating the consequences of one's principled actions.

A NEW TEACHER'S STRUGGLE

Mary Johnson had graduated from college only two years earlier and had recently been appointed to teach 2nd grade in an inner-city school.

The school's student body was notorious for its poor behavior. There had already been three teachers for Mary's class since September, all of whom had left because they could not handle the pressure. Students bragged to Mary that she, too, would be forced to leave and told her that they were "the bottom class" of the grade.

Mary was unused to establishing strong discipline as her supervisor demanded, and this class would have been difficult for the most experienced teachers at the school. Mary neither received the support nor the guidance she desperately needed from the administration in this regard.

Mary had one student in particular who continually acted out. Paul Jones was a born leader, and others in the class looked up to him.

One day students came running into her room to tell Mary that Paul had just urinated all over the boys in the bathroom. It was, she surmised, all "in fun" within Paul's world. Of course, she felt it necessary to call Paul's parents that evening to discuss the incident. When Paul's father heard the story, he put the phone down. She could hear him yell, "Paul, you get over here. I have your teacher on the phone."

Mary subsequently heard the father beating Paul. "What have I done?" she thought to herself as she tried in vain to get the father to stop.

The next day, Paul came into class, smiled at Mary, and said, "Hey, 'teach,' you really got me beat up this time!"

Discussion Questions

1. Did Mary have some other course of action she could have pursued before calling the parent? Could the consequences of her discussion to call have been anticipated? Did she do the right thing?
2. What should Mary do now?
3. Young teachers and inexperienced teachers face special difficulties in controlling their students. How should schools help their new faculty cope with these problems?
4. Do parents have the right to beat their children?
5. Is this a case of child abuse? Should Mary report it?

THE CASE OF THE TAUNTED LONER

Mike was a loner. He kept to himself and had his own unusual style in clothes and music. Academically he did reasonably well, though his work was unpredictable and tended be sloppy.

It was his junior year. Mike was in an art class with some sophomores who took delight in taunting him. The art teacher, Ms. Smith, always supported Mike in what was obviously a one-sided battle. The attacks did not take place during the class but rather before it started or as the students were leaving. Ms. Smith asked her colleagues, and it seemed that Mike was generally the butt of a lot of negative feeling from his upper-school peers.

Ms. Smith decided to talk to Mike, but found him unresponsive. The bully sophomores were similarly uncommunicative.

One Monday Mike found that someone had "accidentally" spilled paint on his current project. His book bag was mysteriously emptied on the floor. The next day Mike came dressed in black leather boots and a black leather jacket, and had a menacing air about him. The other students took one look at him and taunted him unmercifully.

Ms. Smith was just coming around the corner when Mike produced a knife from his pocket. "Just leave me alone, all of you," he raged. "I'm sick of this. I'm not going to take it anymore." The other boys cowered away, shocked and scared. Ms. Smith had arrived just in the nick of time. She told Mike to give her the knife, which he did without protest.

Ms. Smith then took Mike to the upper-school office to face his punishment.

Discussion Questions

1. Should Ms. Smith have acted more strongly in Mike's defense?
2. What should Mike's punishment be? Should the other boys be punished?
3. To what extent can school personnel be expected to recognize signs that any student may become harmfully violent?
4. The clique-forming high school years can be excruciating for students left on the fringes. How should schools address this issue?

"GENTLEMAN'S D"?

Willie Passim had taught high school English for 7 years but had never had seniors before now, his 1st year at this school. Having heard much about "senioritis" from his new colleagues, he was determined not to let it compromise the integrity of his course. On the one hand, Passim sympathized with the students; he could still remember marking time his own senior year in high school. On the other hand, Passim was now at a small community-oriented school with high academic standards. Passim couldn't expect as much of this class as the juniors or sophomores, however, so he made the tests easy enough to pass as long as students came to class and took notes.

While most of the students came to class, wrote the papers, and studied for tests, there was one exception. Claude Pitts had been at the school since 1st grade and had been a C student. He was not involved in any extracurricular activities, unless you counted smoking cigarettes on a nearby stoop. Passim wondered how and why this boy would go to college next year, but he was rumored to be going somewhere. Claude's mother was on the board of trustees and had given many hours of her time to the school, not to mention a fat check each year.

During the first semester Claude had cut class twice and had a D average. He was referred to the school psychologist, but continued to be drowsy in class. Claude's parents didn't come to teacher conferences this year, but Passim reported Claude's work on the anecdotals.

Claude failed the final exam with a 35 after walking out half an hour into the test. He didn't hand in two of the five papers; his second-semester average was clearly an F. No matter how Passim worked the numbers, Claude failed senior English for the year. Passim knew that this meant Claude wouldn't get his diploma or walk up the aisle with his class on graduation day.

Passim wasn't sure what to do. He felt sorry for Claude, and wondered if other teachers had been carrying him along all these years. After all, Claude was barely passing his other subjects and perhaps those teachers were giving him a "gentleman's D." However, Passim was worried about getting grief from the administration, who would certainly be under pressure from the parents if their child did not graduate after 12 years in the school.

Discussion Questions

1. What should Passim do given the background of this situation and the potential consequences?
2. If Passim leaves the F, should the dean overrule him?
3. What should the dean say to the parents?

PROMISES, AUTHORITY, AND STUDENT LIVES

The whole issue of ethical behavior seems abundantly clear to me when considered in the abstract. Our responsibility as teachers is to act in the place of parents; we are mentors, adults, friendly but not friends. Schools structure clear lines of authority so that decisions and responsibilities are easier to make and easier to carry through. Sooner or later, however, life kicks in and the structure that has been set up to clarify situations becomes cloudy and inadequate.

I was in my 4th year of teaching, but as I had started teaching late, at age 26, I was past the age of youthful arrogance when I felt I could, with my enthusiasm and commitment, solve the problems of the young on my own. I was a homeroom teacher for a 10th-grade class, which was rambunctious and lots of fun. Most days I felt like I was driving a chariot spirited by five horses, so great was the energy emanating from the room. Susan had been looking quiet for a considerable time and her friends, her intimate friends, clustered about her. As she went out of the homeroom she slipped me a note, scotch-taped shut, with "Private" written in capital letters across it. In a desperate handwriting, she wrote that she was pregnant and terrified. Her parents, who were West Indian and very strict, would disown her, and she feared being pregnant and abandoned. Could she please talk to me, but most of all, could I please not tell anyone. Of course, I immediately took her from her class and took her to an empty room. What went on there is probably self-evident. There were tears, and all the ample evidence of a young girl not ready to be a mother, one, in fact, sorely in need of her own parents. And they, not surprisingly, were the biggest unknown. We talked, and she accepted that her parents would have to be informed. I offered to do it by myself, or with her, or allow her to tell them before the school talked to them. She asked for the right to do it herself, in her own way, by early evening. The school could telephone after that. I agreed, and then when she left I went to the dean of the Upper School, showed him the letter, and repeated the conversation and promise made to Susan. He listened and said he felt that was appropriate. To my horror, two hours later, Susan was gone from school. Her parents had been immediately summoned and informed of their daughter's pregnancy by the dean and the headmaster. Susan was then brought in and faced her parents. Family and family pride are very important within the West Indian community, and their pride had been taken from them by that bald confrontation. Susan never returned my phone calls, and her friends no longer trusted me or the school. I felt enormously betrayed.

Several years later, another girl came to me. She was taking heroin and was in over her head. She had bought it at a bar and taken it with friends thinking she could keep it under control. Her mother, I knew, was a prostitute, and Monica was really the staple of the family supervising, her younger siblings, including cooking and cleaning for them. In tears, she explained she wanted to be off the drug, but she desperately wanted to finish her schooling, which meant taking her exams in 2 weeks. She feared that if she went to the school, they wouldn't give her the 2 weeks; but equally, she didn't want to wait to talk to me until after the exams, because then school was over. She wanted to make something of her life, and finishing school was the most important component of that possible success.

Should I have gone to the dean of the Upper School and the headmaster with Monica's dilemma? They were the same ones who had let Susan down so terribly. They had stood by their decision when I asked them why they had summoned Susan's parents without telling her or at least letting her see them before the administrators talked to them. They made it clear that I had behaved appropriately in passing the problem to them and that my responsibility and concerns should end there. But it didn't. Susan was a real girl with a real problem, and for good or ill, the ladder of responsibility didn't end my feelings or moral responsibility for the school's involvement in probably the most significant episode in her life. What, then, should I do for Monica? In what direction did the arena of loyalty lie? Was my belief that the school would simply ignore Monica in favor of the larger school's health sufficient to bypass my sense that this, as with Susan, was a defining moment that could be ignored only with significant consequences for Monica?

Discussion Questions

1. Did the dean and headmaster have the obligation to call Susan's parents? Did the teacher have the authority to make her promise to Susan? Did the dean and headmaster have the right to override the teacher's promise?
2. Is Monica's case sufficiently different to justify a different response by this teacher? What would you do if you were the teacher in this situation?

FREEWARE

"I don't mind. I want you to have it."

"Rob, I appreciate the offer, but I can't."

"Why not?"

"Because I'm your teacher. It wouldn't be right for me to accept computer software without my paying for it."

"But I want you to have it. Everybody does it, kids and adults. You should, too."

"Again, I really appreciate the offer, but I have to think of what kind of message I would be sending you if I did something like that, something that is basically illegal."

"But I don't care. And I won't tell anybody about it."

"Rob, I have to think about what kind of example I'd be setting for you. I can't take the software."

That wasn't easy.

Rob was offering to give me software worth over $500 at no cost. He was a computer genius, and his parents always bought him the latest software.

Not that I couldn't have used it, either. I'd just put a new laptop computer on my credit card. At 18% annually, I would spend more than $500 on interest alone as I paid the thing off.

Rob, for his part, had grasped that my constant call for excellence and pride in his work sprang from concern about what kind of man he would become. Like every teacher, I had hoped that my message might seep into the brains of at least some of my glassy-eyed 8th graders, who much preferred talking with their best friends about last Friday night or the 8th-grade trip week that was still weeks away. And, like more than a few of the students in 8th-grade world geography, Rob soon began to put in the necessary hours of research, proofreading, and revising in order to get that A.

His offer of the free software was his way of saying "Thank you." My accepting that offer might have lessened the character of a young man who I believe will do great things at Berkeley Carroll and in life.

Discussion Questions

1. Do you think the teacher did the right thing by not accepting Rob's gift of gratitude?
2. If "everybody does it," doesn't that make this a very minor infraction?
3. Do you think this was really a character-building lesson for Rob?

RACISM? OR JUST TEASING?

Sonia James, a 2nd-grade teacher at a small independent day school, tried to teach her students to be sensitive to the feelings of others and to express their own feelings honestly. She prided herself on instilling respect for people of all races, religions, sexual orientations, and backgrounds. Halfway through the year, she read a biography of Martin Luther King Jr. to the class, along with portions of his "I Have a Dream" speech. She then had the children write their own speeches using King's as a model.

During recess a few days later, Ms. James heard one of the white students, eight-year-old Sammy Smith, run up to the only African-American boy in the class, eight-year-old Jack Williams, and say, "I have a dream that one day we won't be in the same class." The two boys had been in the same class for three years, but were not friends. Sammy continued, "I have a dream, I have a dream, I have a dream," and Jack told him to "Shut up."

Ms. James separated the two boys and made Sammy sit out for the rest of recess. Sammy protested that Jack should have to sit out, too, since he had said, "Shut up." The next day Sammy's parents wrote Ms. James a note, asking her why Sammy had been asked to sit out. They argued that he had only expressed his honest feelings about Jack, and Jack had not been punished for being rude.

Ms. James wondered if she had overestimated Sammy's sophistication and had wrongly inferred a racial taunt in the bantering of two children who didn't like each other. Sammy was often rude to others in the class, and she couldn't be sure that Sammy was not just up to his usual taunting.

A day later, Jack's parents wrote a note to Ms. James expressing outrage that the racial taunts to their son had been punished so lightly.

The last note she got was from the principal, asking her to attend a meeting with all four parents.

Discussion Questions

1. Did Ms. James overreact in punishing Sammy? Did her desire for inculcating children with respect for people of all races, religions, backgrounds, and sexual orientation make her overly sensitive? Or did she in fact underreact and not treat the taunting seriously enough?
2. Assuming Ms. James was correct in her assessment of the situation, what should she have done?
3. How deeply should schools engage in such "sensitivity training"? Should students be punished for being insensitive? Should schools develop codes identifying the difference between sensitive and insensitive behavior?

ON BODY IMAGES

Robin Bloomberg was a 6th-year physical education teacher at a private school, the only female PE teacher for 6th through 12th grades. She frequently discussed health and fitness issues with her students, attempting to provide her students with every opportunity to pursue their own athletic interests and to strengthen their self-images. She is keenly aware that body image is a sensitive issue for adolescents, especially girls.

During the spring, Robin took her classes to a nearby park for physical education classes. Students wore shorts and T-shirts because of the warm weather, and one day during a 7th grade class, Robin noticed that Marsha Chase, one of her students, had numerous black and blue marks on her legs and arms. Robin had previously observed that Marsha had begun to lose weight. Robin waited until the class began walking back from the park to ask Marsha if they could meet privately to discuss "something." Marsha was hesitant at first, but finally agreed to the meeting.

Later that day, Robin discussed her observations with her department chairperson and the middle school director. She told them of her suspicion that Marsha might be anorexic or being physically abused. After a lengthy meeting, it was also decided that Marsha's parents would have to be called about the situation after Robin and Marsha met.

The next day, the two met privately. After several minutes of light conversation, Robin casually mentioned to Marsha that she noticed bruises on Marsha's legs and arms and asked how Marsha got them. Marsha avoided looking at Robin and mumbled something about not knowing. Robin said she had also noticed that Marsha had lost a considerable amount of weight and asked about her eating habits. She also again inquired about the bruises and asked if she was being mistreated. She told Marsha that if she needed to talk about anything, she should feel free to come to her. Marsha said nothing and then said she had to leave for a class.

Discussion Questions

1. Marsha's bruises could be a by-product of her body image problem and her weight loss or abuse, but many other possible scenarios exist. When Marsha refuses to discuss the matter with Robin, how can she pursue it, given that she has no direct knowledge of abuse or an eating disorder? Should the parents be called? Should the school administration get involved?
2. What should Robin and the school do now?

DID SHE CHEAT?

Mr. Edison taught English at an urban independent school. He had been a faculty member at the school for 10 years, during which time he had established a reputation as a demanding teacher and a hard grader. Mr. Edison prided himself on the high standards that he set for his students and was confident that students who measured up to these standards would be well prepared for the challenges they would encounter in college.

Mr. Edison taught a variety of upper-school literature courses. The primary method of evaluation in each was the analytical essay, in which students were required to argue a point of view using sound logic and appropriate examples drawn from literature. To give students an opportunity to demonstrate that they had done the assigned reading, Mr. Edison also devised and administered multiple-choice tests that asked students simply to recall factual information about literary characters and plots.

Teresa Bledsoe was one of the weaker students in Mr. Edison's senior course on the American novel. Teresa was no lover of literature and had enrolled in the course only to fulfill the school's graduation requirement in English. Although she had occasionally demonstrated some insight in her writing, Teresa's work in the course was generally of poor quality. As the school year drew to a close, it was apparent, both to Mr. Edison and Teresa Bledsoe, that Teresa would need to work hard to pass the final exam in order to earn credit for the course.

Teresa's final exam paper was one of the first that Mr. Edison read. Much to his surprise, Teresa earned a score of 88 percent on the multiple-choice section of the exam. The score was 25 points higher than any other score that Teresa had received. Perhaps, Mr. Edison surmised, Teresa had finally taken the course seriously. Much to his disappointment, however, he found no evidence of such study when he turned his attention to the two essays that Teresa had written. Both were very poor, providing the reader with only a few obscure generalizations. The details that Teresa had recognized on the multiple-choice section of the exam were not cited.

As he considered this discrepancy, Mr. Edison's suspicions were aroused. He began to wonder whether Teresa had copied the multiple-choice answers from a fellow student. He decided to ask the exam proctor, Mr. Karmen, if he had noticed any suspect behavior during the exam. When questioned, Mr. Karmen confessed that he had spent much of the exam period reading *Sports Illustrated.* Mr. Karmen did at least manage to recall where Teresa had been seated during the exam: alongside Heather Ellis.

Heather was Teresa's best friend. She was also the top student in the class. Determined to get to the bottom of this disturbing business, Mr. Edison confronted the two students with his suspicions. Teresa denied that she had cheated. When asked to account for the disparity between the score of 88 and the scores in the 50s and 60s that she customarily earned, Teresa insisted that she had studied. Heather claimed to be unaware of any cheating. When asked if she had helped Teresa during the exam, Heather denied that any collusion had occurred.

Mr. Edison wanted to believe that Teresa's score of 88 was the result of serious study, and without a confession he had no proof that it was due to cheating. Furthermore, Teresa had been adamant in her denial. To press further on the matter, by calling home or by involving a school administrator, would be to challenge not only Teresa's honesty but her competence as well. Perhaps, Mr. Edison reasoned, it would be best at this point to simply let the matter drop. If he did this, Teresa would pass the final exam and with it the course.

Discussion Questions

1. Cheating can be a thorny issue, especially when a teacher does not witness the cheating directly. To what extent should a teacher pursue suspicions of this nature? Do you think Mr. Edison handled this situation fairly?
2. What options does Mr. Edison have to determine whether Teresa was cheating? How much evidence is required to warrant punishment?
3. To what extent should Mr. Edison consider the emotional well-being of the students involved in determining his course of action?
4. Mr. Edison has a dilemma of academic integrity versus potentially false accusation. Which should weigh more heavily on his mind?

A VIOLENT CHEATER

Bob Gorfman was a 1st-year science teacher in a large department at a major independent school. As a new teacher with three courses of his own, he also had been assigned to serve as a teaching assistant in a unique departmental course designed for all seniors. His duties included teaching a few sections, grading homework, and proctoring tests, while the head of the department, Dr. Shirky, gave lectures. Every now and then there were reports of cheating on tests, but Bob was generally very good at monitoring students during exams.

The night before the final exam, Bob received a phone call from one of the students, Linda, who asked to remain anonymous. She knew that some students were planning to cheat on tomorrow's exam, and although she wouldn't divulge their names, she wanted Bob to know. Bob thanked her for the information, and chose not to tell Dr. Shirky about the phone call in order to preserve Linda's anonymity.

Instead, Bob took extra precautions to protect against cheating. He went to the classroom an hour early to separate the desks, and he marked the back of each blue book with a small green ink dash in one corner. When the exam started, he walked down every aisle, making sure that all the students knew they were being watched.

Sure enough, at least one student was cheating, and Bob caught him. Freddie, a B+/A- student, had seemed particularly nervous every time Bob walked by, and suspicious movement on Freddie's desk caused Bob to take a closer look. Bob spotted an extra blue book and pulled it off the desk, much to Freddie's consternation. The blue book was unmarked, and contained pages of equations that the students were supposed to have memorized.

Bob brought this blue book to Dr. Shirky across the hall, who admonished Freddie but allowed him to continue taking the test. Dr. Shirky told Freddie that disciplinary measures would be taken.

Dr. Shirky recorded the incident in Freddie's permanent school record, and his senior science course grade was reduced to a C-. Bob thought his responsibilities were at an end; after all, as a new teacher and serving here merely as a teaching assistant, he had no control over the administration of the departmental course. His only role was to report the incident.

But then Linda and other students came to Bob to protest the light punishment given to Freddie. Apparently there was much more to the story. Freddie had not only cheated constantly throughout the semester, but he had a violent temper and more than once had threatened other students with physical harm. Although Freddie had no direct evidence that someone had fingered him for cheating, he was convinced that someone had and was planning to find out who it was. Linda and the other students believed that Freddie was dangerous.

Bob asked them what they expected him to do, given that he had no control over the administration of the course or the department. Linda and the others asked him to report Freddie's behavior to the dean, but didn't want to get involved themselves because they were afraid of Freddie. Bob pointed out that the head wouldn't be able to take action unless someone actually testified as to Freddie's behavior, and that Bob himself couldn't because Bob hadn't witnessed anything but cheating. He volunteered to accompany Linda and the others to the head office, but they refused. They seemed to feel that it was Bob's responsibility to take care of Freddie, and to protect their anonymity as well.

Discussion Questions

1. What should Bob do? If you were a teacher in a similar situation, how might you approach Freddie, keeping in mind his violent and vengeful tendencies? Should you go to the school's head alone?
2. What should be the school's action concerning Freddie? Do you agree with Dr.Shirky's solution? Should schools have stated policies for dealing with academic dishonesty?
3. How can a school react when one of its students is reputed to have threatened other students?

Illustration by Katie Kennedy-Gately, Grade 7

3

Teacher/Administrator Cases

Schools are organizationally structured to provide for the education of students. The primary role of teachers is instruction, and the primary role of administration is leading, managing, and serving the entire school's population in the support of instruction. Administration, broadly conceived, includes not only school heads, principals, department chairs, and so forth, but also such support staff as counselors, librarians, and consultants. The spheres of power are clear: administrators are in charge of the school and its support functions, and teachers are in charge of their classrooms. Sometimes however, their powers overlap and clash. Sometimes, administrative directives on curriculum conflict with the teacher's view of what and how to teach. It is no wonder, then, that many ethical dilemmas arise in the context of the teacher administrator relationship.

In this chapter a number of ethical issues arise in the cases from such situation as pressure to revise a student's evaluation, lack of follow-up in a suspected child abuse case, unwelcome sexual advances, copyright law, student punishment, religion in the classroom, parental pressures, classroom management, and a supervisor's advice for improvement.

A REPORT CARD DILEMMA

Ms. Chester was a new 2nd grade teacher. One of her students, Mike Foster, was a child of a parent who contributed considerable time and energy to the school. Mike was a fine student who was liked by his peers. Ms. Chester thought highly of Mike's work throughout the year, and this had been reflected in conversations with the parents and in Mike's first report card.

Mr. Davis, the school's lower-school director, was familiar with Mike because of his dealings with his father. He often chatted with Mike in the halls, the cafeteria, and in the playground.

In June, Ms. Chester submitted her end-of-the-year report cards to Mr. Davis for his review. Ms. Chester had put much time and thought into each report card, and her hard work was evident. Mr. Davis, however, suggested revisions on her anecdotal comments, asking Ms. Chester to strengthen her language regarding Mike's ability. Ms. Chester's anecdotal comment began, "Mike is a capable math student who shows interest in his work. He understands math patterns and concepts and is willing to practice those skills which are more challenging." Mr. Davis wanted her to change the opening sentence to read "Mike is an excellent mathematician!"

Ms. Chester was surprised and frustrated with this "suggested" revision.

Discussion Questions

1. How should Ms. Chester proceed? Imagine various scenarios and their potential consequences. What would you have done if you were Ms. Chester?
2. How could Mr. Davis have handled the situation better?
3. Can such changes in student records be justified?
4. Most independent schools rely heavily on their students' parents. How does this reliance affect equity? Are there any ways to mitigate this situation?

UNFOUNDED SUSPICIONS?

The annual science fair was the highlight of the academic year in the science department, although it was also a time of great tension and anxiety for teachers. Each of the students did a project, which was evaluated by their teachers, and then about 150 of the best projects were chosen to be displayed at the fair. All students had to write a paper as part of their project, so in addition to putting on the fair and running classes, science teachers had to read a major assignment from each of the students. So Mr. Barnes was already weary when he started to read Wilma's paper. He was also a very young teacher, and he was still inexperienced in many of the challenges teaching would present to him.

Wilma was in 7th grade, and she was a good student. Though not exceptionally bright, she was willing to work, and was quite eager to please her teachers. She was quiet. She loved doing labs, not so much because of a passion for science, but because it gave her an opportunity to work and talk with her friends. She was the shortest girl in the class, and her stature made her shy; labs presented good opportunities to overcome her shyness.

For the science fair project, Wilma had chosen to report on child abuse. She had done well on her project, having researched the topic thoroughly. As Mr. Barnes read the paper, he was pleased with her use of sources. The paper included very little that wasn't already well known to Mr. Barnes, but there was little to criticize about the work. Then Mr. Barnes read the last sentence: "Sexual abuse can be very damaging to children, and can even lead to stunted growth."

Mr. Barnes had never heard this before, and was highly skeptical that there was a proven link between sexual abuse and shortness. But he could not ignore the fact that Wilma herself was the shortest girl in her class. He was at a loss about what to do.

The next morning he went to the library and borrowed all of the books mentioned in Wilma's bibliography. He was sure that none of the books would mention a link between sexual abuse and stunted growth, but if he could find such a factual link, he wouldn't need to confront the implications of Wilma's belief that such a link existed. Of course none of the books mentioned a link. But now he did not know what to do.

Mrs. Simpson, the school psychologist, was a good listener, so Mr. Barnes photocopied Wilma's paper and went to Mrs. Simpson's office. The two of them talked for about 30 minutes. They agreed that Mr. Barnes's suspicions of sexual abuse were probably correct, and that Wilma was probably asking for help by putting such an obvious clue at such a prominent point in her paper. They also agreed that this was a very difficult situation to deal with: The evidence of abuse was flimsy, confronting the parents would very likely make the situation worse, and bringing the authorities in could be disastrous. They also agreed that Mrs. Simpson was probably in a better position to deal with the situation than Mr. Barnes was. Needless to say, Mr. Barnes did not nominate Wilma's project for the fair.

Mr. Barnes thought a lot about the situation during the next several months, but he didn't talk to anyone else in the school community about it until the end of the year, when he visited Mrs. Simpson again. She hadn't yet decided how to deal with the situation.

Discussion Questions

1. To what extent should teachers feel responsible for seeing clues to abuse? Once teachers believe they have seen such clues, what should they do?

2. Mr. Barnes obviously would be unhappy that the school counselor has taken months to take action on Wilma's perceived call for help. What should he do now? Could the counselor be considered negligent, especially if sexual abuse is in fact occurring in Wilma's home?
3. Should Mr. Barnes speak directly to Wilma about the final sentence of her paper?

UNWELCOME ADVANCES

Marie, a young African-American teacher in her 1st year of teaching in a suburban private school, was leaving an assembly one day when she felt a hand firmly resting on her buttock. She quickly turned around and behind her was Ed, an African-American junior in her English class. Ed was a quiet young man and had already made her uncomfortable by coming to work in her classroom during free periods, where he spent much of the time simply watching her. When approached, he would say he was thinking. Uncertain as to whether the touch was inadvertent or deliberate, Marie opted to say nothing, but felt uneasy. The next week, in roughly the same circumstances, the same thing happened. When she turned and saw Ed, he merely stared at her. This time she felt certain that the incident was a deliberate action. She felt angry that this was happening, but uncertain as to the best way to handle the situation.

She told Anne, who was the dean of students. Anne's first instinct was to call the parents, without first discussing it with Ed. First, however, she and Marie went to George, who was dean of the upper school. Upon hearing the story, George said, chuckling, "Oh, I think he has a crush on you."

Marie felt abandoned by both responses. She felt belittled by the upper-school dean's response, interpreting his remark to be an indirect way of saying she was overreacting. She felt that Anne was taking a route that would be confrontational, thus making the situation difficult to resolve. She also felt that she was betraying Ed because they were both members of a very small ethnic group within the school. She felt she should be able to deal with it herself, but then felt angered by the inappropriate touch.

Discussion Questions

1. What should Marie do now? Should she talk to colleagues? To Ed? To the parents?

2. How should the administrators have reacted? Were they appropriately supportive?
3. Does the fact that Marie and Ed are both part of an underrepresented group in the school have an influence on how the situation should be handled? What if the two had been of different races?
4. Students often harbor crushes on their teachers. How can schools prepare young teachers to deal with these emotions?

TO COPY OR NOT TO COPY?

JoAnne has been a librarian for 15 years and runs a very active program. She meets with teachers regularly to plan for research projects and to keep abreast of curricular progress. She encourages teachers to bring their classes to the library. She encourages teachers to use various media both as teaching tools and as reporting instruments for students.

Video editing machines fall within her area of responsibility. While she encourages use of the machines, JoAnne makes every effort to educate her colleagues and the students about copyright laws and insists that they follow proper practices. From time to time, teachers have consulted her about making copies of hard-to-find videos either from their personal collections or from someone else's. She has consistently used these incidents to remind her colleagues of copyright infringement.

Teachers generally seem to understand and respect JoAnne's position on copying principles, especially as it relates to videotaping. One day she was approached by Brenda Isaacs, a Spanish teacher. Brenda planned to attend a weeklong conference and wanted to show the same film to each of her four classes while she was away. Brenda decided that they should make three additional copies of the videotape and didn't think it would be a problem since the school owned the videotape. When JoAnne objected, citing copyright violation, Brenda offered to erase the copies at the end of the week when the substitute completed her assignment. JoAnne voiced her objection but offered to investigate and clarify potential copyright violation in such a circumstance.

A week later, JoAnne happened to see three copies of the videotape in question along with viewing instructions for the substitute teacher on the secretary's desk. JoAnne was upset and pondered what her course of action should be. As the person in charge of the media center and its services, she feels obligated to protect the school's interest by adhering to proper copyright standards, but she is not eager to sour her relationship with Brenda.

Discussion Questions

1. Copyright laws are seen by many teachers as an annoyance. How important is it for schools to follow them? Should the school ask at what point does reproduction of copyrighted material become truly criminal? Or should the letter of the law predominate in all instances?
2. How should JoAnne handle her dilemma? Should the fact that Brenda acted without awaiting JoAnne's final advice change JoAnne's thinking?
3. Do actions such as Brenda's adversely affect the ethical standards of students?
4. What does "fair use" mean in copyright law as it pertains to educational uses?

HOW TO DEAL WITH VIOLENT REACTIONS

Ms. Davis is a social studies teacher at a public high school. She is a 20-year veteran of the school and a former member of the board of education in the school district in which she lives. Ms. Davis has always been regarded by her students as fair and evenhanded in dealing with both academic and disciplinary issues.

Due to an excessive number of unexcused absences, senior Eric Watkins was in danger of failing Ms. Davis's class. If he failed, Eric would not graduate with his friends in June, and he would have to repeat the class during the summer school session. In an apparent effort to improve his academic standing, Eric decided to attend classes on a regular basis and develop an independent study routine at home.

At the beginning of a class period, Eric asked Ms. Davis if he would be able to borrow a copy of the class textbook so that he could study at home. Due to the school district's current budget crisis, the high school was not able to purchase enough textbooks for Ms. Davis to distribute a copy to each of her students. In an apologetic tone, Ms. Davis told Eric that the shortage of books prevented her from lending copies of the book to students for use at home, but that he could borrow a copy during his lunch period when she was to meet with a small class.

Eric became visibly angry and insisted that since his parents paid their taxes, he had a right to borrow a textbook. Ms. Davis apologized again and told Eric that she couldn't change her policy in fairness to the other students. Eric became violently angry and swore at Ms. Davis. Ms. Davis told Eric to leave the classroom and to report to the dean of students. At the end of the class period, Ms. Davis wrote a report of the incident for the dean.

At the end of the school day, Ms. Davis learned from the dean that Eric was punished with one day of detention for the incident. Ms. Davis was shocked by the lenient punishment and decided to report the incident to the school principal.

The next morning, the principal informed Ms. Davis that Eric would receive a two-day suspension from school. When Ms. Davis questioned this decision, the principal said a longer suspension was not reasonable since the number of Eric's unexcused absences from school would then exceed the legal limit and that Eric would be required to repeat his senior year.

Discussion Questions

1. Considering all the circumstances of this case, did the principal make the correct decision regarding Eric's punishment? Should Ms. Davis have allowed Eric to borrow the book overnight?
2. Would a longer suspension have served Eric better?
3. Suppose the school's student handbook stipulated a specific punishment for violent behavior. Should that policy then be followed in all cases? How heavily should written policy weigh in decisions of punishment? Can cases exist in which policies should be modified or abandoned?

PARENTAL PRESSURE

Willy Wiseacre has been a student at Brooklyn Institute since preschool; he is currently a senior in the high school. Willy is a good student, talented artist, and all-around athlete, but his attitude leaves much to be desired. Willy is rude, disruptive in class, and irresponsible. He is late daily and often misses homeroom and the beginning of first-period class. For this behavior he has received numerous detentions, but is blase about the consequences, which are minimal. Moreover, Willy's mother has been notified repeatedly of her son's antics, but little has changed.

Willy's mother is a prominent lawyer and member of the school board who contributes her time and money generously to the school community. Mrs. Wiseacre has been in touch with Mr. Socrates, Willy's English teacher and adviser, by telephone on numerous occasions.

Yesterday, Mrs. Fairminded, the senior math teacher, told Mr. Socrates that she would no longer teach Willy unless his behavior changed. "Frankly," she told Mr. Socrates, "the administration and Mrs. Wiseacre can go to hell!" Blushingly, Mr. Socrates suggested that Mrs. Fairminded speak with Mrs. Wiseacre. Mrs. Fairminded said that she had tried but was told by Mrs. Wiseacre that Willy was merely being a boy, acting immaturely, and would be graduating, so she was not too concerned.

Mr. Socrates went to Mr. Whippit, the new upper-school head, conveyed Willy's current situation and his history, of which Mr. Whippit was aware, and suggested that action be taken. Mr. Whippit, having set a tough but fair tone this year, summoned Willy and Mrs. Wiseacre in for a meeting concerning this ongoing problem. Mrs. Wiseacre refused to attend and gave tacit consent for her son to ignore the conference. Willy was suspended. Mrs. Wiseacre had a fit and contacted the headmistress.

After conferring with Mrs. Wiseacre over the phone, the headmistress suggested that Mr. Whippit withdraw the suspension because of the potential harm that could arise, with a possible lawsuit, poor publicity in the community, and emotional damage to Willy, who would be graduating in May. With hands tied, Mr. Whippit got back to Mr. Socrates with this administrative dilemma.

Mr. Socrates advised Mrs. Fairminded of this touchy situation. In effect, Mrs. Fairminded was left with the final decision concerning Willy. She could either live with Willy as he was, or she could switch him into another class.

Discussion Questions

1. Should Mrs. Fairminded shift her responsibility on to another member of the math department to the detriment of other students?
2. Should she confront the administration about this matter and threaten her resignation if Willy is not held accountable?
3. Should she let Willy back into her class, grit her teeth, and live with him until graduation?
4. Do you think the administration handled this case in the best possible way given the circumstances? Why or why not?

RELIGION IN THE CLASSROOM?

As a new French teacher, Mr. Michel, began an introductory course in an elementary school, he had few worries that the cultural differences between America and France would cause any serious problems. In the teacher's experience, the differences between French and American cultural traditions were well accepted by the American population. After all, France and the United States are both stable, democratic countries with huge technological and scientific industries. Their citizens enjoy freedom of speech and religion, and both nations recognize the separation of church and state.

After Mr. Michel had taught his 4th graders the numbers up to a thousand, the months, and the way to give the date, he then wanted to teach them how to say the years by giving them a historical context. To help him, he had an excellent children's magazine with humorous characters and pictures of objects, giving the dates when various objects were created. The dates started in the years BC. The children seemed to enjoy the lessons and their French vocabularies improved dramatically. As with every lesson, the children received with their homework a list of the vocabulary in French translated into English.

A week after the initial lesson, a parent complained to the school director that the teacher had been improperly promoting his religion because he had used the phrases "Avant Jésus Christ" and "Aprés Jésus Christ" to translate BC and AD. He had also presented a French calendar which, like most French calendars, included the Catholic saints' names.

The director agreed with the parent and told Mr. Michel there was to be no further reference in class to the religious aspects of French culture. But, the teacher pointed out, Christianity and Catholicism are integral parts of French culture, history, and the language itself. Seemingly convinced, the director agreed to let the teacher decide for himself what to teach, but secretly worried what the complaining parent and others would say about the French lesson at Christmastime!

Discussion Questions

1. It can be very difficult for teachers to recognize issues that may offend some members of the community. How can schools ensure that their curricular offerings are seen as unbiased? To what extent should schools concern themselves with such issues?

2. The teacher here chose to present dates in their most widely
    accepted format. Is the fact of their predominance enough to jus-
    tify their teaching?
3. If schools were to banish all mention of issues associated with a
    specific religion (or race, or gender, or any other group), what
    effects would this have on the curriculum? What if the school
    were to do the opposite, that is, to try to balance all teaching
    with summary views of many beliefs?

FALSELY ACCUSED?

Right out of college, Aaron Smyth had been chosen from a group of
very solid candidates to fill a slot as English teacher at a prestigious
boys' school in the South: his energy, obvious intelligence, and personal charisma greatly impressed the English Department chair, and
the demonstration class Aaron taught as part of the interview process
was outstanding.

Aaron arrived on the conservative school's campus very much
more liberal than his posture during the interview, but was well
received and appreciated, especially by the students. Storm clouds
began to brew, however, by his 2nd year, when a boy in his class
objected to what he perceived to be a continuous antiestablishment
polemic in the teacher's curriculum. The pot boiled over when the
student's parent showed the head of school an exam essay, purported-
ly a grammar exercise, that was taken from an antimilitary tract.

Just at this time, the English Department chair secured a position
as head of school at an all-girls' boarding school. Since he had a high
opinion of Aaron's teachings and had himself been guilty of the same
sort of youthful excess due to inexperience in some of his early years
of teaching, he was happy to bring Aaron with him to his new school.

Very shortly Aaron became both very popular with his students
and somewhat controversial with his peers because some faculty saw
this young teacher as far too close and familiar with his charges. His
wife, who began teaching drama at the girls' school (part-time) and
raising their young children (full-time), was seen by the whole community as an incredibly talented teacher and drama coach and as a
real asset to the school.

By the end of Aaron's 3rd year, he had been promoted to chair of
the English Department and College Counselor—and in the latter role
worked very closely with all the girls in the junior and senior classes.
The one and only official blemish on his record at the school was an

indication from a mother that her daughter had felt that while Aaron was doing a lights-out midnight check on his duty night, he had hugged her to console her over a disappointment, and the hug had seemed to the girl to be too intimate. After a conversation with the dean and the head, Aaron had reassured both that his intentions had been honorable and that he would be especially careful in the future. Nonetheless, the event was worrisome, since so many girls seemed to have a crush on the teacher (which of course was flattering to him) and spent (some thought) much too much time with him privately.

Disaster struck at the end of year four when a highly gifted girl, active in drama and creative writing, wrote a "fictional" story that presented having an affair with a young, married English teacher. The story was graphic and detailed. As the girl's teacher, then adviser, then the dean and finally the head probed, she flatly denied that the verisimilitude of the story had any basis in fact. At the same time, she was telling friends (and giving explicit details of times and places) that she indeed was having an affair with Aaron. And her friends were absolutely convinced that she was telling them the truth and lying to the school authorities.

The problem for Aaron was that the other girls were not only persuaded of the affair but they also persuaded their teachers, so in effect the entire community soon had convicted the teacher of a crime he most likely did not commit and feared that the head would turn a blind eye on the situation to protect a favorite.

In extensive conversation with the head of school, Aaron convinced the head that he was innocent of the accusations: the head both believed the protestations of the teacher, knew that there was no factual support for the accusations, believed the girl had been truthful to the school authorities, and knew the girl was exceptionally capable of creating a fiction that could cause havoc in the community. Unfortunately for Aaron, the damage to his reputation was very real in the community, and the atmosphere there had become poisoned.

Discussion Questions

1. To what extent is Aaron responsible for the situation?
2. Was his viability as a teacher and community member so compromised as to make it impossible for him to continue at the school?
3. What should the head do under these circumstances to be both fair to the teacher and responsive to the school community?

THE BEST EDUCATION MONEY CAN BUY

Ms. Rice, a 1st-year teacher at an Eastern boarding school, has among her students the son of an extremely wealthy board member who has just pledged to donate $3 million toward a new library. Unfortunately, De Haven Sanson Jr., while an affable 10th grader and star soccer player, is no Spanish student. His first quarter mark is a C-, and the anecdotal report sent home reflects his teacher's concern that if De Haven is having this much trouble mastering introductory material, the road ahead will indeed be rocky. There is no response from De Haven Sanson Sr. As the year progresses, the son's grades continue to wane in Spanish, and after failing a midterm examination and subsequent F's for both the second and third quarters, Ms. Rice arrives at the end of the academic year and must submit a final grade. The student shall receive an F.

The department chair, who has been "monitoring all language grades from the outset of the year," makes no comment when De Haven's failing grade is reported. In fact, he jokes that for all the money the family possesses, the son is "pretty much of a dope."

Two days later the department chair returns to speak with Ms Rice. He asks if there isn't some way De Haven might receive a D-rather than an F. The chair adds that the very fate of the massive building project may depend upon this young man's grade in Spanish. He also mentions that the head, a close friend of the father, has taken a personal interest in the matter and is quite displeased at the prospect of "this fine young man failing Spanish." Ms Rice attempts to justify the decision, citing past anecdotals in which Haven's poor study habits and disastrous test scores were enumerated, along with entreaties made by the teacher and housemaster for the boy to seek help. Suddenly the department chair grows misty-eyed describing what a marvel De Haven is on the soccer field—a veritable Pele—and how many students could benefit from the new library as well as the attendant positive publicity the school would receive.

Taking the student's great personal and athletic attributes into account, Ms Rice decides to give the student an F anyway. One week later, after all grades have been submitted, she happens to be checking out the grades of some of the boarders, and decides to see what other grades have been garnered by De Haven, since there was surprisingly little conversation about him.

When Ms. Rice finds the transcript of final grades, she sees that De Haven has received three D's and three C's. The F given by the Spanish teacher has been changed to a D-. There is, of course, no notation by the grade to indicate how or when the grade was altered. Ms. Rice immediately goes to the department chair to see if he knows anything about the grade change. He professes ignorance and suggests Ms. Rice drop the whole issue.

Discussion Questions

1. This case clearly puts a teacher in a difficult position: she feels betrayed by her school, and she must feel severe injustice in De Haven's final grade. What should Ms Rice do?
2. Assuming the source of the grade change was the school's head, how should the teacher proceed?
3. If, as the department chair suggests, Ms Rice does "drop the whole issue," what are the short-term and long-term ramifications of the grade change on the various constituents of the community?
4. Should Ms. Rice tell her colleagues of the grade change? Should she tell anyone else? What would happen if she did?
5. Children of trustees often seem to receive special privileges at independent schools. Is this just a fact of life we have to live with, or can or should something be done about it?

BUT IS IT PLAGIARISM?

Bill Gulliver was a star on the varsity swim team and the son of a trustee at a prestigious day school. He had a diagnosed reading disability and struggled to keep up in a demanding history course taught by the young and intense Mr. Nigel. Only a few months into the school year, Bill turned in an important term paper. Mr. Nigel sensed the material had been plagiarized right away: there was a complexity to the writing and arguments that Bill had not produced before. Mr. Nigel counseled Bill to submit his own work before the final due date, but the final draft came in largely unchanged. When Mr. Nigel demanded to see Bill's sources, his suspicions were confirmed. Several passages were taken straight from the sources, with only superficial alterations. This seemed to be an open-and-shut case of plagiarism at a school with a well-established honor code.

Bill's parents took offense at Mr. Nigel's claim, indicating that he had not seen to their son's special needs early enough in the process of researching the term paper and that Bill had acted out of desperation and frustration. They complained to Mr. Nigel's principal and the school's head, expressing anger that a school they had taken great pains to shape had "devastated" their son out of the "negligence" of a young teacher.

The typical process in such cases at this school would be for Bill to stand trial in front of the Honor Council, a highly regarded student group that made strides to educate students before and after mistakes. Punishments for guilty verdicts were usually meted out by school administrators. All in all, the system was effective, swift, and taken very seriously in the school community.

The head, after hearing Mr. Gulliver's complaints, postponed Bill's Honor Council trial in order to meet with Mr. Nigel and, as he put it, "get the facts straight." Mr. Nigel was livid that administrative pandering to the interests of a trustee threatened to undermine both his authority as a teacher and the academic integrity of the school.

Only a few minutes of the meeting with Mr. Nigel had elapsed when the head reminded the young teacher of Mr. Gulliver's standing in the community. The head asserted that the ramifications of this case "could really bring the roof down."

Mr. Nigel questioned his superior: what did he mean by "bring the roof down?" Would school close? Would Mr. Gulliver resign from the board and refuse future donations? Would Mr. Nigel's job be in jeopardy? Mr. Nigel contended that to let such an act go unpunished would be a disservice to Bill and to the school. The meeting ended in a stalemate.

The head decided to suspend Bill for the following day. Other plagiarism cases had had stricter penalties, but this case was softened because Bill was considered, in the words of the head, "a nice kid who doesn't get it yet."

Mr. Gulliver complained that an important league swim meet was scheduled on the Thursday of the suspension. Bill had been tapering his training schedule to get particularly fast times, and the father felt that the school had again been inconsiderate of his son's needs and talents. The head changed the suspension to Friday and Bill swam successfully at the meet on Thursday.

Discussion Questions

1. Heads of school feel many pressures. If we may assume that the head involved in this case led a school for which incoming funds were necessary and scarce, and that Mr. Gulliver would cease his giving if his son were to suffer academic sanction, what should the head have done?

2. If you believe the head erred in his response to this scenario, what were his mistakes?
3. All schools develop policies for dealing with academic dishonesty. Once written, when might it be appropriate to follow a different course of action? Considering all of the priorities at work here—the student's, the school's, the teacher's, the head's, and the parents'—was the decision appropriate?
4. Schools serve students first and foremost. How would the incidents of this case affect Bill? How would they affect the rest of the student body?

ALMOST COMPETENT

Tom Brady is the head of the middle school at the Parkchester School, an urban independent school with an enrollment of nearly 800 students, located in a recently gentrified area of the city. The majority of the children in Tom's division come from the immediate neighborhood. While the school's parent body included a good number of lawyers and a smattering of financial types, many parents were writers, artist, filmmakers, teachers, or professionals who had moved to the neighborhood to escape the high cost of living elsewhere in the city and to live in a neighborhood that had a small-town feeling in the middle of the big city. The school prided itself on the high level of parental involvement in school activities and had an open-door policy of welcoming parents at school events and of soliciting parental feedback. Well-educated, articulate, and always mindful of the money they were spending to send their children to private school, Parkchester parents were never shy about letting Tom know their opinions of any topic of importance to them, from the issue of homework (too much or too little) to their perceptions of various teachers.

Early in the school year, one of the first parent concerns Tom had fielded had been from a 6th-grade parent complaining about her daughter's new history teacher, Susan Bishoff. New to the school that year, Ms. Bishoff had had a year's experience teaching at a small boarding school for emotionally disturbed boys before coming to Parkchester and, despite having taught a rather tepid demo lesson, had received very strong recommendations from her former head of school. While Tom had been reluctant to hire a teacher with only a year's experience—and none with middle schoolers—his choices had been limited. Ms. Bishoff's previous experience, Tom reasoned, would surely help her deal with the usual classroom management problems that young teachers invariably face with middle schoolers, and her department chair and mentor, both strong veteran Parkchester teachers, would provide her with all the curricular guidance she might need. Yet here it was the third week of school, and already there was a parent on the phone complaining about—of all things—Ms. Bishoff's classroom management problems, specifically her inability to handle the rambunctious boys in the class.

Coincidentally, Tom had just had a conversation with Ms. Bishoff about a situation involving these boys. She had approached him in tears following a class in which, during a game of "history charades," some of the boys, including the son of the vice president of the school's board of trustees, had made some crude sexual gestures toward the girls in the class, such as moaning and wiggling their pelvises. Calling the four boys "hooligans," Ms. Bishoff wanted Tom to take some disciplinary action. Privately thinking that this was the sort of behavior that middle-school boys are known for, Tom called the boys' parents, gave them all after-school detention, and demanded that they write letters of apology to Ms. Bishoff, which they did. It was not long after this that Tom received the phone call from a girl's mother complaining that Ms. Bishoff had no control over the boys in the class, and not long after that Tom received another phone call from the parent of one of the boys, not the board vice president, who accused Ms. Bishoff of hating boys.

Needing to see for himself, Tom visited Ms. Bishoff several times over the next several weeks. What he saw was evidence of solid lesson planning, but many of the usual new teacher mistakes in putting good plans into action. She had some classroom management problems and was often unclear in her explanation of an assignment, nothing, he thought, that couldn't be improved with additional mentoring and supervision. When he offered her suggestions, he found Ms. Bishoff somewhat defensive, again referring to the boys as hooligans. Thinking the best way to reach her might be through her department chair and mentor, both women, Tom approached them and offered his observations about how they could help her improve the clarity of her presentation and her classroom management. They agreed to meet with her daily to plan lessons and to observe as many classes as they could.

By December, parent ill feeling toward Ms. Bishoff had gotten worse. Tom was now fielding weekly phone calls from parents about everything from her talking down to the kids to her complicated assignment sheets. Visiting the classroom again, Tom saw that few of the changes and suggestions that he, her department chair, or her mentor had discussed with her had been implemented. He had expected this, as both her department chair and mentor had said that despite their almost daily work with her on lesson planning, she seemed bent on resisting suggestion and making mistakes for herself. They found her pleasant and polite, but ultimately difficult to work with, since she would not take direction. In his own observation of her classes, he saw that the children seemed to have lost respect for her, frequently talking while she was talking, or worse, not talking at all, even when asked a direct question. And yet, once again, Tom couldn't pinpoint anything more severe than the usual beginning-teacher problems.

By the end of January, Tom had heard of a meeting that had taken place one evening at the home of a parent of a child in Ms. Bishoff's class. Most of the parents from Ms. Bishoff's class were in attendance, and the topic of discussion was how to salvage the year. A good number of parents had already hired private tutors because they felt that Ms. Bishoff was not teaching writing properly. (Tom had, in fact, talked with her about a stack of uncorrected papers from November he had seen on her desk recently; Ms. Bishoff had said that was the only assignment she had neglected to correct quickly.) Other parents advocated demanding that the school administration replace Ms. Bishoff with a more experienced teacher in midyear. (Tom had thought of that, but knew that an experienced middle-school history teacher was not easy to find in January.) Other parents said that unless something was done, they might consider finding another school next year.

Following a meeting with the PTA grade representatives, during which the details of this parent meeting came out, Tom considered his options. He was certain that Ms. Bishoff was not a good teacher and was certainly not cut out to teach middle school, which required more patience and humor than she seemed to have; he had, in fact, decided not to offer her a contract for the next year. Yet she was covering the curriculum, not as well or as fully as the other teachers, but from Tom's observation, learning was going on. Plus, he thought, she did have some rambunctious kids in her class who were occasionally disruptive in other classes, although not to the degree they were in hers. In light of this, some of her difficulties were understandable. And yet, through it all, she seemed strangely resistant to take any suggestion from Tom, her department chair, or her mentor, or to make any changes in her teaching.

Tom had finished pondering his options when, a week after his meeting with the PTA reps, he came to school early one morning to find a petition in his mailbox from all the students in Ms. Bishoff's class demanding a new history teacher and, on his voice mail, a message from the vice president of the school's board of trustees that her son was the one who started the petition, that she was well aware of and supported his circulating it, and that if something was not done immediately about her son's placement in Ms. Bishoff's class, she would withdraw him from the school next year.

Discussion Questions

1. Where do Tom's primary obligations lie: to the teacher, to the parents, or to the students? Can he balance these obligations? Should he try to balance these obligations?
2. What message might he be sending to the faculty if he dismisses Ms. Bishoff in midyear? To the students? To the parents? What message might he be sending to the faculty if he does not dismiss Ms. Bishoff in midyear? To the students? To the faculty?
3. Tom does not have a replacement in mind should he dismiss Ms. Bishoff. Should having a good replacement in the wings make a difference in his decision?
4. On what ethical principles should Tom base his decision?

Illustration by Zachary Dresler, Grade 3

4

Teacher/Parent(s) Cases

The old Latin phase, in loco parentis, *is used less and less to describe the role of school as standing in the place of the parents with regard to its students. Not all, but many parents more and more feel a great responsibility to shepherd their children through school, and their main direct contact with the school is through the teacher of their child. Very often, teacher and parent views are at odds with one another, and many ethical issues can arise in such a context.*

Cases in this chapter deal with issues regarding such things as grading practices, racial composition of classes, politicizing the curriculum, an alcoholic parent, parent role in helping to control a student's disruptive behavior, disagreements about what constitutes proper behavior, parental pressure for extra help versus fairness to others in the class, and loyalty to the school versus possibly appropriate parental criticism of the school.

AN ODD PARENT–TEACHER CONFERENCE

Ms. Bailey was 6 hours into the fall parent–teacher conferences. She was tired, her mouth was parched, and she was two appointments behind schedule. Seated beside her was Mrs. Benjamin, a parent of a middle-school student. Looking through her child's essays, the mother turned to the teacher and said, "You know, you grade my son way too leniently. He's got to fail a few times to get his butt in gear. There's no reason to give him a B. He doesn't deserve it."

Ms. Bailey was a bit flabbergasted. After taking a deep breath, she reviewed Dominic's work with Mrs. Benjamin, pointing out the things that he had done well and mentioning the things she wanted him to work on during the term ahead.

"Basically, what I see is that Dominic can't spell for beans," said Mrs. Benjamin. "Look, this is wrong, this is wrong, and this is wrong. When I was in school, my teachers took a letter grade off for each spelling mistake. If you only pushed him on this, penalized him for his mistakes, then maybe he'd learn something. The way you do it, he'll never get anywhere."

The room was silent for a few moments. Ms. Bailey could hear the parents for the next appointment chatting at the door.

"Tell you what," blurted the mother. "Give him a C- next time, if he makes this many spelling mistakes, just to see if he gets it in gear after that. That couldn't hurt, could it?"

Ms. Bailey knew that she had to wrap up the conference quickly, so that the schedule didn't fall too far behind. She told Mrs. Benjamin that while she, too, was concerned about Dominic's spelling, she couldn't decide upon a grade before a paper was written.

Mrs. Benjamin got up to leave. While opening the door and within earshot of other parents, she said to Ms. Bailey, "I thought you were interested in helping my child learn."

Discussion Questions

1. Should Ms. Bailey have pursued the conversation? How should she address the situation, and with whom—just Mrs. Benjamin? other faculty? administrators?
2. What, if anything, should be said to the parents who overheard the conversation?
3. Schools feel considerable pressure concerning grades from parents, but not usually from parents who wish their children's grades to be lower. Should teachers and schools ever cede to such pressure? Should Ms. Bailey consider grading Dominic based more on spelling? Is it possible not to consider the issue while reading his papers in the future? Could Mrs. Benjamin be right?

CULTURAL IDENTITY

An African-American couple, Mr. and Mrs. Blake, carefully selected a relatively small private school for their three children. The school prides itself on its multicultural curriculum and its sensitivity to the needs of its diverse student population but does not consider ethnicity in its classroom-placement decisions.

The Blake's oldest child entered 1st grade with four other students of color in a whole class of 60. By random chance, the four other children were placed in the same class, making the Blakes' daughter, Alicia, the only student of color in her class. Alicia loved her teacher and got along well with the other children in the class.

During their first meeting of the year, Mrs. Blake told the teacher that Alicia had mentioned being the only black child in the class several times. The Blakes were worried about Alicia's developing identity and her feelings of difference. The Blakes and Alicia's teacher were unsure of how to handle the situation, and so they decided only to communicate often and do their mutual best to help Alicia feel a sense of belonging.

Alicia's teacher feels torn in this situation. Although Alicia never mentions any problem in school, she can see that Alicia is often moody or depressed. Alicia often complains of stomachaches, and cries for no apparent reason. Though she does not know if these problems are attributable to Alicia's sense of her own difference, the teacher wonders if it is fair to place one child of color in a class alone if there are other alternatives.

Discussion Questions

1. Should children of color be placed together for identity development reasons?
2. Should the process of class placement continue to be "blind," or should the school more carefully assess class lists before the school year begins in order to ensure ethnic balance?
3. Should parents of color be consulted in the process? What if two sets of parents disagree? What would the school's overriding policy be?
4. If Alicia's parents and the school decide to leave Alicia in class, how could the teacher help Alicia feel more comfortable? How should a teacher of young children—or a whole school of young children—approach the issue of race?

WHOSE VIEWS ARE THEY?

Even the youngest students can understand current events on some level, and so a 1st-grade teacher decided to talk in simple terms to her class about Iraq's invasion of Kuwait and the ensuing 1991 Desert Storm conflict. Eventually the teacher displayed to the community a letter that all her class had signed and then sent to President Bush. It was apparent that the words in the letter were the words supplied by the teacher. The letter called Operation Desert Storm an immoral war and branded U.S. soldiers who fought immoral. Parents did not find out about the letter until after it was sent to the White House and a copy was displayed on the school's bulletin board.

The teacher was popular and had taught in the school for over 10 years. She was a hard worker who cared about her students. But some parents (including some who supported the teacher's view of Operation Desert Storm) were outraged that she had used the 1st-grade classroom as a forum for proselytizing her political views. Some parents said that such proselytizing showed insensitivity toward any young children who had relatives fighting in Operation Desert Storm. They wanted the school to censure her in some way that preserved her job but let her know officially that her letter was inappropriate and that some limits governed her classroom teaching.

Discussion Questions

1. Most teachers and school administrators would agree that academic freedom for teachers is essential. At what point, though, does academic freedom overstep reasonable bounds?
2. Should current events be discussed in school? At what age level is discussion of these events appropriate?
3. How should the school administration handle a situation like this?
4. Should teachers avoid proclaiming their own political beliefs to students? Are there occasions when teachers' opinions can be useful to students' learning?

AN INAPPROPRIATE PARENT

Ms. Hodson, a 1st-grade teacher, was working late one night when Mr. Clark, the father of a little girl in Ms. Hodson's class, appeared in the doorway. She was surprised, but welcomed him to come in. His daughter, Margie, followed. Margie appeared shy but excited by this unusual situation.

Ms. Hodson quickly noticed the distinct smell of alcohol on Mr. Clark's breath and saw that his eyes were reddened. Margie begged for her father's attention; she wanted to show her father some of her work. He paid only slight attention to her as he tried to have a conversation with Ms. Hodson.

Ms. Hodson was alarmed by her perception that Mr. Clark had been drinking and that he seemed to be neglecting his child's pleas.

A couple of days later, Mr. Clark appeared in the doorway again. This time he was alone. He walked right in and sat in a child-sized chair. He talked in a peculiarly serious way about a homework assignment she had given the children a few days before. Once again, he smelled of alcohol and had red eyes. Ms. Hodson felt extremely uncomfortable and found a way to leave the room. As she left, Mr. Clark headed down the stairs to pick up Margie from her afterschool program.

Ms. Hodson told the school director of these two encounters. Some investigation found that Margie's kindergarten teacher and the director of the lower school were aware that Mr. Clark had regularly picked up Margie smelling of alcohol.

Discussion Questions

1. What should Ms. Hodson and her superiors do? Does a school have a right to intervene in a parent's personal problems?
2. How should a school react when a faculty member is subjected to uncomfortable situations by parents of the school's students? In this case, what could have been done to reassure Ms. Hodson?
3. On the rare occasion when a parent engages in inappropriate personal conduct with school personnel, is it wise for the school to remove that parent's child from its community? What about the child's welfare and best interests?

WHOSE RIGHTS TAKE PRIORITY: THE INDIVIDUAL'S OR THE GROUP'S?

Jed was in Sarah Thompson's 3rd-grade class, the first class of her new career as a teacher. Jed's 1st- and 2nd-grade teachers had warned Sarah that Jed was in constant trouble, and on the 1st day of school Jed verified their warning. A boy insulted him and Jed backed the boy into a corner, pressing a pencil tip into the boy's throat. As the days and weeks passed, Jed demonstrated anger on a daily basis by stealing things from other children; kicking, pinching, and punching anyone whom he felt was insulting him; and paying little attention to his teacher's requests and reprimands. Jed rarely smiled.

Jed did his academic work quickly, and his skills were on grade level. He seemed most content when working on very structured, practice-type assignments. The teaching style Sarah had learned while earning her master's degree at a progressive teachers college, however, was oriented to hands-on projects requiring student interaction. Jed rarely got along with classmates long enough to complete a project, and would often destroy his work and the work of his peers.

Sarah believed in dealing with student conflicts and difficult social issues by having meetings with the children involved and teaching problem-solving techniques. When this approach failed with Jed, she called his parents for a conference. The parents were concerned about Jed's school experiences. Jed's father said, "It takes a lot of money to send Jed here, and I want him coming home every day and saying, 'Dad, I had a great day in school today!' But he's not saying that and I want to know why."

When Sarah described some of Jed's negative behaviors, his mother said, "I'll bet those children were all teasing Jed. I don't want my son to be anybody's punching bag. I tell him he's just got to hit them right back!" Sarah said she had not noticed anyone teasing Jed, but that she would watch carefully. She then told Jed's parents that in her classroom physical aggression was not tolerated, and that she had been teaching the children ways to solve their conflicts with dialogue. The conference ended with all participants feeling unsatisfied.

Sarah became more and more concerned about Jed, and so she spent as much of her time with him as possible. She made a special effort to notice and praise his successes and talents. When he misbehaved, Sarah listened to his side of the story and patiently counseled him about better choices for expressing himself. Sarah sensed that Jed was terribly unhappy, and she wanted to help him feel better about himself and become more comfortable with his classmates.

Jed had made some friends. One boy in particular sought Jed's company, but Jed played with him in a domineering, sometimes violent way. The parents of this boy complained to Sarah that he was starting to have mysterious headaches and stomachaches and, on a few mornings, even asked not to go to school. Sarah assured the parents that she would keep Jed and their son as separate as possible and monitor their playtimes.

Soon more parents were complaining to Sarah about Jed. A few parents spoke to the director of the elementary school, complaining that their children did not feel safe in school. Some parents went so far as to threaten removing their children from the school.

The elementary director, Sarah, and Jed's parents met to discuss Jed's behavior. Jed's parents defended their son, adding that they felt that since he was the only African-American child in Sarah's class, he was the victim of a range of racist remarks that Sarah was not hearing. Jed's mother said, "I walk in the building sometimes and people ask me whose babysitter I am. Boy, are they surprised to find out I'm a parent, just like them."

Two days later Jed attacked a child from another class on the playground. He gave the boy a black eye, and when the child fell to the ground, Jed kicked him.

Sarah felt as though she had done all she could to help Jed, and she and elementary director believed they had reached a dead end in dealing with Jed's parents. Though Sarah had pursued the issue diligently and with care, she had come to see no good avenue for resolution of the problems: if Jed were removed from the school, other children would be happier, but Jed's educational interests would not be best served, and if Jed were to remain, Sarah could think of no new approach to make the classroom safe and comfortable for all.

Discussion Questions

1. Often a teacher must balance the needs of one child against the needs of the group. Sarah is concerned about Jed's self-esteem and wants him to develop the social skills necessary to get along with his peers. Meanwhile, Jed is acting out in a way that is intimidating and hurtful to others. Whose rights should take precedence in this case, and why?
2. The perception of parents and the perception of school staff are sometimes at odds. In this case, they directly conflict. Jed's parents advocate hitting as an appropriate response to insult, whereas the teacher is opposed to physical solutions and punishes any child who hits, no matter what the reason. How can these two viewpoints be reconciled?
3. Jed learns best when doing quiet, structured work. His teacher does not like assigning that type of work, preferring interactive, hands-on lessons. When a teacher's style conflicts with a student's learning style, what can be done?
4. Jed's parents raised the issue of race in their conference with the director and Sarah. Sarah had not noticed any racist interactions between Jed and her students, but that does not mean none occurred. What are a teacher's and a school's responsibilities for creating an equitable community for all of its members? How should admissions policy be involved? How should class placement plans be considered? What kind of staff training should be implemented? When an event occurs that involves racism, what systems should be in place for handling it? How, in this case, can we define the boundaries between a child's responsibility for his or her own individual behavior and the effect of pressures brought on a child by racism?

A PUSHY PARENT

Mrs. Tucker is simply not satisfied with her daughter's progress in school. She and her hard-working husband pay very high tuition bills at a popular independent school in an attempt to provide the best possible education for their 10-year-old daughter, Fiona. According to Fiona's early IQ tests, she should be at or near the head of her class. Now, in 4th grade, however, Fiona's math skills lag far behind those of many classmates. Mrs. Tucker is convinced she knows the reason for her daughter's severe problem of underachievement, and so she goes to see the head of the school, Mr. Lloyd, and presents the following argument.

Mrs. Tucker tells the head Fiona's 3rd-grade class was the source of the problem. She believed the teacher to be competent, even skilled, but there were far too many unmanageable, "special-needs" students in the class. Fiona had difficulty concentrating with all of the noise and other distractions in the classroom. Mrs. Tucker believes other children had a detrimental effect on her daughter's academic progress.

Mrs. Tucker believes that tutoring might help Fiona to get back on track in her academics and to gain some much-needed confidence. Mrs. Tucker emphasizes that she and her husband cannot afford to pay a tutor in addition to the tuition they are already paying. And since she believes the school is at fault, she thinks the school should provide tutoring.

After several meetings and phone calls, it becomes clear to Mr. Lloyd that Mrs. Tucker is not going to back down. Something must be done to appease her. Although this is an unusual case, he can imagine that he might have similar feelings if he were in Mrs. Tucker's place. Mr. Lloyd decides that Fiona's current teacher, the young Ms. Thompson, should be asked to provide afterschool tutoring.

Though Ms. Thompson already feels overwhelmed by the task of providing solid classroom instruction for all of her students, she feels obligated to grant the head's request. She does not welcome the idea of spending so much extra time on one particular student when all of her students are equally deserving of her attentions, and Fiona's test scores in class indicate that she is keeping up well.

Ms. Thompson believes that she is being unduly imposed upon. She had nothing to do with Fiona's 3rd-grade experience, but the head has asked her to give her time for free.

Discussion Questions

1. If you were Ms. Thompson, would you refuse the tutoring assignment? Would you accept the assignment, but request payment for your time?
2. Should the school accept the blame for Mrs. Tucker's dissatisfaction with Fiona's academic performance?
3. If the school agrees to provide free tutoring for Fiona, should the school offer tutoring to all students?

4. How should Mr. Lloyd have handled the situation? How can administrators simultaneously protect their faculty and appease the school's parents?

TOO CLOSE FOR COMFORT?

Ms. Johansen has lived in the neighborhood surrounding the independent school in which she has taught for more than 2 decades. When she first began to teach at the school, few of her neighbors sent their children there. In recent years, with the growth of the school's reputation, many of her long-term neighbors, who have become close friends, have enrolled their children in the school. This has meant that Ms. Johansen frequently finds herself in the position of having colleagues who teach children of close friends.

The school is often a topic of conversation at neighborhood social events, putting Ms. Johansen in delicate situations. One particularly awkward moment came when Mrs. Walters, the mother of a 9th grader, complained vociferously about the uncaring nature of the school in its treatment of her son. Ms. Johansen had been at many meetings where Mrs. Walters's son had been discussed. It was the school's belief that Mr. and Mrs. Walters were unresponsive to the school's overtures to work together to help their son improve his academic performance.

At the social occasion in question, Ms. Johansen was put in the position of listening to Mrs. Walters's criticism of the school and silently standing by while knowing there was more to the story. However, she could not respond without revealing confidential and professional information that she knew about the younger Walters's academic situation and his parents' role. Although she was unhappy about not coming to the defense of the school, Ms. Johansen said nothing.

Discussion Questions

1. Did Ms. Johansen have any other options for dealing with this situation?
2. Faculty members often live in their schools' community and, as a result, hear much discussion of that school. Should they engage in or refrain from such discussions?
3. Is it ever appropriate for a faculty member to discuss issues such as the one in this case when off-duty? If so, how should such discussions be handled?

Illustration by Elizabeth Dubois, Grade 8

5

Teacher/Teacher Cases

Most if not all teachers tacitly assume a professional identity that includes a set of obligations, moral and otherwise, to the students, the parents, the administration, the school, and, most importantly, to each other as colleagues. Certain expectations of respect, honesty, fairness, openness, and goodwill are generally presumed in interactions with fellow teachers. Breeches of these expectations as well as perceived breeches of proper professional conduct give rise to ethical issues in the teacher/teacher context.

This chapter explores some typical situations that give rise to such issues as observation of a colleague's mistreatment of students, teachers disagreeing over grading practices, pressure from colleagues to grade a student athlete higher, suspicion that a fellow teacher is having a sexual relationship with a student, and observation of a very unprofessional teaching practice.

A COLLEAGUE PROBLEM

Patty Schroeder was a 4th-grade teacher at a K–6 school in an upscale neighborhood in a major Eastern city. Although many of the public schools in this city faced numerous hardships, including overcrowded classrooms, inadequate supplies, and broken-down buildings, Patty's school enjoyed more advantages than most. It had an active Parent Association, which annually raised thousands of dollars to pay for such extras as an art teacher and visiting staff developers, a talented and gifted program, afterschool activities, and a dedicated and experienced faculty. Many of the students' parents were professionals who showed a deep concern for their children's education and expected a quality education from the school The majority of the students, in turn, were motivated and eager to succeed.

Patty taught a class of 32 students who exhibited a wide range of reading levels, math and writing skills, and maturity. Most were well behaved, but several were disruptive and demanding. After a few weeks, however, Patty had established a smoothly functioning classroom, with clear rules for behavior. Minor incidents occurred almost daily, but Patty was generally pleased with the class and its progress.

The class visited the computer lab once a week. After about a month, Patty noticed that when she announced that it was time for computer class, many students would groan in dismay. When she asked the students why they were reacting this way, one told her, "Ms. Smith, the computer teacher, always screams at us. She tells us we're the worst class in the school, and the stupidest." Another chimed in, "Yeah, and last week she grabbed me by the shirt and threw me into my seat." This statement came from one of the more disruptive students in the class, so Patty asked, "What were you doing before she grabbed you?" The student replied, "I was out of my seat watching Jeremy and Michael play a computer game." Michele, another student, said that a few weeks earlier Ms. Smith had screamed so loudly at Christa, a shy student who was still learning English, that Christa burst into tears.

Patty was disturbed by these allegations, especially the report of physical contact between Ms. Smith and a student. She told her students that they should try their best to behave well in Ms. Smith's class, and to work hard while they were there. She also said she was very sorry that Ms. Smith had yelled at them, and asked them to keep her informed about any further such incidents.

After their session in the computer lab, Patty asked the students how the class had gone, and they reported that Ms. Smith had taught them a typing program with no problems. The following week, during parent–teacher conferences, a parent told Patty that her son hated to go to computer class. Patty tried to reassure the parent that she was looking into the matter, but she told herself that she was really not handling it properly. After the next computer class, Jessica, another student, approached Patty and told her that she had overheard Ms. Smith speaking in the hall to another teacher saying, "Jessica has had such an attitude from the very first day. I'd really like to smack her." Patty tried to assure Jessica that Ms. Smith wasn't serious about her threat of physical harm.

Patty believed that the situation was getting out of control, and although she knew she should discuss the situation with Ms. Smith, she was reluctant to do so. Ms. Smith was the head of a committee that chose teachers to teach summer school courses. Patty had applied for one of the summer school positions, and she was very eager to get it; she needed the extra income to finish her graduate degree. Patty knew that competition for the summer school teaching positions was fierce, and she was fearful that if she confronted Ms. Smith about the incidents in the computer lab, Ms. Smith would hold it against her and deny her a position. At the same time, Patty was concerned that her students were being taught by someone with a bad temper who seemed unable to control her anger.

Discussion Questions

1. The quality of the professional relationships among teachers in a school is vital to the efficient running of a school. Teachers must feel that they can discuss issues such as curriculum, student behavior, and management strategies with each other in an atmosphere of trust and mutual respect. Given Ms. Smith's authority over the decision-making process regarding summer school teachers, was Patty's concern about pursuing the matter with Ms. Smith justified? Should she have discussed the issue with another teacher first, or perhaps have gone straight to the principal and requested her intervention?
2. Did Patty react appropriately when the students first told her about Ms. Smith's behavior? How should a teacher respond when students complain about another teacher's performance or actions? Regarding the overheard conversation between Ms. Smith and another teacher, what guidelines should teachers follow in general when they are discussing students during the school day and possibly within earshot of the children?

FACULTY MEMBERS AT ODDS

Mr. Quibble and Mr. Street have been uneasy colleagues for several years at a small independent school. They are both in their forties, have both taught for 20-plus years, and have been working in the same department for 3 years. Mr. Quibble is the senior member of the staff. He considers the maintenance of academic standards his most important function in the school. Mr. Street (whose nickname among the students is "Easy" because he is undemanding in class) views the affective side of education to be at least as important as the intellectual training the students receive. He believes in "holistic education."

At the end of the first marking period, one of Mr. Street's students from the previous year approaches him. The 11th grader, Peter Boyo, did very well with Mr. Street in 10th grade. Street commended Peter for his "creative and imaginative approaches to problem-solving" and his "independent thinking and flair for self-expression." To Street's consternation, Boyo informs him that the latter's grade in Quibble's class is likely to be an F. Boyo shows Street several assignments, copiously marked in red by Quibble. When Street peers through the red marks, he sees a pedantic focus on detail with no attention paid to either the content or the form of Boyo's work. He decides to talk with Quibble about the matter.

The conversation is not a success. Quibble seems to Street to be stiff and unyielding in his demands and rigid in his thinking, even with a colleague. Quibble refuses to consider allowing Boyo to redo the assignments on the grounds that it would be unfair to other students who do not have the same opportunity. He reiterates his belief in "high standards."

As the second marking period progresses, Street becomes more and more convinced that Quibble is making Boyo a target of disapproval, low grades, and excessively high expectations because Street challenged him. Boyo's parents complain to the dean of students but are told that nothing is demanded of their son that is not expected of all other students. The parents are aiming for a highly competitive university for their son, but Quibble says that he would be doing the student no favor by lying to him about his abilities.

Street begins to suspect that the student may be caught in the middle of a clash between the two teachers. A talk with the dean has no effect; the dean tells Street to clear up the matter with Quibble by himself and seems annoyed to have been brought into the problem. The dean tells Street that all students have problems with Quibble, that he is a demanding teacher, and that the dean likes it that way.

Discussion Questions

1. There may be as many different concepts of evaluating students as there are teachers. To what extent should schools attempt to codify expectations in this realm? What is the effect on the faculty of carefully prescribed grading guidelines?
2. How should Mr. Street pursue his quibble with Mr. Quibble?
3. Can you imagine a case in which a student suffers as a result of friction between two faculty members? If so, how should such a situation be addressed?
4. How can high academic standards coexist peacefully with schools' increasing desire to educate children holistically?

ATHLETIC PRESSURE

A new French teacher at a suburban private school was charged with a class of 33 students. One of the students in that class, Jonnie Baimbridge, an outstanding baseball player and candidate for a college athletic scholarship, had serious difficulty in French in the beginning of the second semester.

He was a senior and was doing so poorly that Mr. Lemieux went to see Jonnie's guidance counselor and asked him to speak to Jonnie about the seriousness of the situation. Two or three weeks passed and no improvement occurred. Soon the teacher had a visit from Jonnie's baseball coach; he expressed his concern about the situation, especially because Jonnie's eligibility to play baseball on scholarship at Carmel University depended on him passing his French class.

A week later, Jonnie, to whom his coach and his guidance counselor had spoken, was still failing French. The second semester was drawing to a close by then, and one afternoon Mr. Lemieux had a visit from the coach and the guidance counselor together. In no uncertain terms, they told the teacher that it was in everyone's best interest to pass Jonnie in French, regardless of his overall results. The tone of their voices was stern, and Mr. Lemieux felt threatened.

They added that there was no point in referring the matter to the principal since he would undoubtedly send back the problem to the guidance counselor for a solution, and we all know what that solution would be.

Discussion Questions

1. Mr.Lemieux is in a bind. His integrity is obviously threatened, but so, he may perceive, is his employment. To whom should he turn? What other options does he have? What should he do? How can he justify his decision?
2. What he should do seems clear: he should fail Jonnie. But would a teacher in such a situation be able to do that?
3. How do sports and their athletes affect the ethical fabric of a school's academic quilt? Should schools lessen their impact?

A RUMORED AFFAIR

Ernest White was in his 1st year of teaching math at an urban independent school. Ernie had been hired for a 1-year position to replace a faculty member who was on sabbatical leave. He was determined to do well and was hopeful that a more permanent position in the department might open during the course of the year.

Teaching in the upper grades seemed to suit Ernie well. Students, parents, and school administrators all had a good feeling about him. Only very recently graduated from college, Ernie still remembered what it was like to be a teenager and seemed to have a knack for relating to students. Many students often took advantage of afterschool time to chat with him.

Shortly before the Christmas break, Ernie had one of these afterschool conversations with Daniel Smith, a 12th grader. The conversation strayed to information that troubled Ernie greatly. Apparently a good friend of Daniel's, a student named Desiree Rogers, was having a sexual relationship with one of Ernie's math department colleagues, Lou Shanks, a 7-year veteran of the school. Moreover, Daniel said that he witnessed the two of them "kissing over open books" through a tear in the poster that covers the window on the door to Lou's classroom. Daniel said that he was scared telling the story to Ernie but did so because he was concerned and didn't know what else to do.

Discussion Questions

1. What should Ernie do? Is it appropriate for him to confront Lou Shanks? Desiree Rogers? his department chair? an administrator? the headmaster? Is it advisable or appropriate for him to try to get Daniel to do one or more of the above? Addressing such a situation can be very difficult. What are the ramifications of Ernie's various options?
2. Teachers usually find dealing with contentious issues with students far easier than dealing with such issues with their colleagues. How should a school's administration help to make sure difficult collegial dilemmas are handled well?
3. Rumors can be devastating, and rumors regarding sexual affairs seem to cling to young, accessible faculty members. How can this problem be addressed?

A BAD EXPERIENCE OBSERVING A COLLEAGUE

As a relatively new teacher, Ms. Martin was excited about her opportunity to observe her colleague, Ms. Williams, who had been teaching at the school for many years. Though Ms. Williams had some very creative ideas and a wide body of knowledge, Ms. Martin found her lesson disorganized. Her teaching was disrupted largely due to her lack of control over the children and her inability to manage the room effectively. Like most teachers, Ms. Martin has had classroom management struggles on occasion, but she was very disturbed by Ms. Williams's comments and responses to the children's behavior. Ms. Williams often yelled, told children they were "being bad," and offered inappropriate rewards for the few children who followed her rules. Most of the children seemed bewildered about what was expected of them. The class period was chaotic, and when the children left to go to another room, they seemed frustrated and acted rowdy.

Ms. Martin was upset by what she'd seen and was confused as to how she should proceed.

Discussion Questions

1. Ms. Martin believed strongly that her colleague was unprofessional in the classroom, but she feared both telling others and confronting Ms. Williams. How should she handle the situation? Given that Ms. Williams is the more veteran teacher, should Ms. Martin ignore the problem she perceives?
2. Suppose Ms. Martin were to approach the divisional director and ask her for advice concerning the situation. Should she broach the topic by allowing Ms. Williams to remain anonymous? Could she affect any change simply by asking the divisional director about the administration's classroom observation policies? Should schools implement formal, ongoing teacher-review policies? At what point do such policies intrude on teachers' academic freedom?

TOO PERSONAL?

Discussion in Mr. Boyer's psychology classroom sometimes becomes very personal, and the teacher believes such sharing enlightens all of his students. At those times when the talk becomes most private, Mr. Boyer takes the role of listener.

On one occasion recently the students turned to the television show *Beverly Hills 90210* and how the characters on the show were dealing with their relationships. The conversation led to talk about relationships in general. At some point during this conversation, students mentioned that a teacher of theirs had told a class that sex with her partner was not very exciting. This led the students to a discussion of how they felt about this teacher and the disclosure, and many revealed that they found the disclosure inappropriate and upsetting. Mr. Boyer was stunned and not quite sure how to respond.

Discussion Questions

1. Classroom discussions of a personal nature often veer toward the uncomfortable. Is that a good reason not to engage in such discussions?
2. Mr. Boyer faces a dilemma. Given that he knows the teacher in question, what should he do?
3. Student–teacher relationships are a cornerstone of independent schools' environments. When do such relationships become inappropriate? Should students know anything about their teachers' personal lives?
4. Sexuality is a topic much on the minds of upper-school students. How should schools address the many issues associated with it? What are some of the most difficult issues to deal with? Why?

Illustration by Andrew Farrell, Grade 6

6

Parent(s)/Administrators Cases

Being an administrator often demands more than carrying out the routine tasks that keep the school functioning smoothly. One area sure to raise problems, however, is the parent–administrator relationship. Sometimes parents make demands; sometimes they fail to act in the best interest of the child. Sometimes administrators lack flexibility in their dealings with parents; sometimes they disagree with how children are being treated at home.

The cases in this chapter consider ethical dilemmas that arise in such situations as parents demanding a change of teacher for the child, parents questioning retention in grade of their child, parental religious beliefs clashing with school policies, parents misusing school lists of names and addresses of other parents, and differing views of the proper treatment for a student with anorexia and another with a serious attention deficit disorder.

A DIFFICULT PARENTAL REQUEST

It was early September. New preschool children were being "phased in" to their school, which means that children were coming into the class a few at a time until the entire class was admitted. This phasing-in process usually takes 3 days.

A 3-year-old girl was phased in the very first day, and school administrators were pleased to see that she separated quickly and easily from her parents—she ran right into the classroom with nary a look back. The teacher knelt beside her and with a warm smile said, "Hello Rebecca." Rebecca seemed happy; the parents said good-bye, and off they went. Rebecca continued to be happily engaged through her first morning. She played with puzzles, listened at story time, had snack with the other children, inspected her new surroundings, and played in the "housekeeping corner"—in short, Rebecca participated fully in the class. When her parents returned at noon to pick her up, Rebecca ran to them with a smile on her face and gave them a big hug.

The following day the parents dropped off Rebecca and then proceeded to the admissions office, where they vehemently demanded that Rebecca be moved to another class, claiming they did not like Rebecca's teacher.

The director responded by explaining that the classes had already been formed, that each class had 18 children with an appropriate balance of boys and girls and a good mix of ages. Rebecca's parents persisted; eventually they threatened to pull the girl out of the school if Rebecca could not change classes.

When the parents left, the director of admissions sought the advice of the divisional director. The divisional director argued against moving the child based on the following points:

- Much time and careful thought had been put into forming the classes;
- Rebecca was in a good grouping with wonderful peers, an experienced teacher, and an assistant teacher;
- Rebecca had enjoyed her first day;
- The parents would come to know and respect and appreciate this teacher;
- The school cannot begin to grant every parental request; and
- The teacher would feel a lack of support from the administration.

The admissions director supported moving Rebecca on these points:

- Rebecca would not upset the gender or age balance in the other class;
- Flexibility in dealing with such issues is good and rarely harmful to the school;
- Rebecca's first teacher could be in for a long year if the parents of one of her students were predisposed not to like her; and
- When the parents are happy, the child is happy.

The divisional director prevailed, and Rebecca never returned to the school.

Discussion Questions

1. School administrators often face parental requests whose implementation would in some way disrupt the balance of the school. How can administrators reach decisions that suit the entire community? Which administrator above offered the sounder argument?
2. Under what circumstances would it have been appropriate for the divisional director to move Rebecca to a different class?
3. Which is more important: flexibility, or backbone?

SHOULD A SCHOOL PROMOTE A PRESCHOOLER?

At the end of March, the parents of a child enrolled in a private school's preschool division were advised by the child's teacher, the division's director, and the division's child psychologist that their child would benefit from another year in preschool. The administrators based their recommendation on their independent observation of the child's work and his interaction with peers and teachers.

The child's parents were unwilling to accept the school's recommendation. They argued that it was possible that their child would rise to the challenge of keeping up with children in kindergarten, who were slightly older and more mature than he. After much discussion, the parents offered a compromise that was accepted by the school administration. The child would be placed in kindergarten in the fall and if, after 2 months, it was determined that he was not meeting the challenge, the school would then place him in a preschool class.

Discussion Questions

1. The youngest of a school's students can in many ways be the most demanding. How should a school approach the difficult task of placing students in the most appropriate grade level?
2. What problems could be caused by the compromise the school struck with the parents? Who will determine if the child has met the challenges? How should the school avoid such "middle roads" in the future?
3. The child's best interest is, of course, the primary concern of his parents and the school. Why, then, do the adults' views so often differ? How can schools uphold their integrity while serving every student well?

MEDICAL TREATMENT AND SCHOOLING

Last year there was a 1st-grade student, Tom, whose mother was a Christian Scientist. She was an educated, intelligent, and articulate person. Her instructions concerning her son were clear and explicit: no medications, immunizations, physical exams, psychological testing—no medical interventions under any circumstances. She left the school the number of their Christian Science practitioner, whose prayers the mother believed to be both preventive and curative in the case of illness or injury.

Along with others in his class, Tom contracted chicken pox. After recovering and returning to school, he still had a few pox scabs. A few of these scabs on the side of his neck had become infected and were puffy, red, and oozing. He exacerbated the condition by scratching and rubbing the area. The infection could have spread and become systemic. With most children, the nurse would have routinely cleaned the scars with antiseptic and dressed them with an antibiotic ointment. With Tom, however, the nurse cleaned the site with soap and water and applied hot compresses. Sepsis never developed, but the nurse had been worried that Tom's scabs could get far worse.

Discussion Questions

1. When religious beliefs conflict with the mainstream medical community's treatment procedures, which should take precedence? What if the child were carrying a highly infectious condition? What should the nurse do if the child were, say, stung by a bee and proved to be violently allergic to bee stings? Was the nurse's treatment of Tom a "medical intervention," which the parent forbade?
2. How much medical treatment should schools be expected to provide? How much medical advice? Should medical treatment of any kind be part of an educational institution's responsibility? If yes, on what grounds? If no, why not?

MISUSE OF SCHOOL INFORMATION

At Litchfield School, we distribute to parents class lists with addresses and telephone numbers of students and their families. These are distributed with the consent of all people involved and with the intent to enhance communication between families. Over many years it has always worked well, as the information was treated with courtesy and appreciated for the efficiency and community it created.

One year, however, a phone call came in from a parent sharing distressing information he had learned through a casual meeting with other parents. A father who also had a child in their children's class had, on at least three separate occasions, gone to classmates' homes to ask parents for financial assistance because of a car breakdown. He explained that his wife and child were in the car. The tow truck was on its way but would not tow them unless paid in full. The father said he did not have sufficient funds in his wallet to pay for towing. He explained that the class list was accessible in the car and so realized another school family lived close to where the car had stalled. Each parent, of course, was able to relate to this father's concern for his family and willingly gave him the amount of money requested or more to help him through this emergency.

But now it was apparent that the father's story had to be a hoax and a manipulation to secure money for some unknown purpose. The caller asked the school's administrator to intervene so other parents would not also be taken in. All parties involved were from one class and surmised the father would continue this practice for the same purpose until he depleted all the names. Their biggest concern was not so much the amount of money they had each handed over but how this man was using the school information.

The school had already been notified confidentially that this father and his wife were separated. The administrator, although hesitant, called the wife's home. Upon hearing the news, the wife was not surprised and explained that her husband had major problems he had to get under control. She was quite disappointed that he had infringed upon their son's school community. She was also upset that he had involved her and their son in the story. The administrator advised, and she consented, that as a means of protection for their child and other parents, the mother would write a letter to the group without disclosing details, as that would infringe upon her husband's privacy. She wrote that she and her husband had been legally separated and it had been brought to her attention that a story was going around about her family's need for emergency financial assistance. Her message was that this was an untrue story, and others should see it as such.

The decision and action taken meant that limited but personal information of one family had to be conveyed to others in order to protect the parent body and to curtail this father's unrestrained use of the list for his own purposes. We later learned there were several more families who had also been approached by this father. The wife's voluntary cooperation and her letter brought the unfortunate situation to closure.

Discussion Questions

1. Are the school and administrators responsible for the misuse of the information that the school has provided to parents?
2. Has the deceptive father committed a crime? Should he be reported to the authorities?
3. Should the mother be put in a situation in which she must share a private matter, her separation, with other parents? Was there any other possible solution to this problem that would avoid this potential embarrassment?

ANOREXIA AND RESPONSIBILITY

As a school head, Jon have been monitoring a problem of a student going through what must be referred to as anorexia. While the condition, at present, seems to be responding to therapy and the combined efforts of school, parents, and friends, there are long-term ramifications. The fact that the girl is gaining weight at the moment does not necessarily represent a cure. And to add to the problem, the therapist has yet to meet on any regular basis with the parents, preferring to meet only with the girl. The parents think things are under control. Everything I know about psychology, therapy, and eating disorders tells me that this kind of treatment is not what virtually all professionals recommend. How does a school head intervene here? Jon has tried to speak with the parents, but they trust the therapist and believe that they are getting results. They are, to some short-term extent. However, the parents are often in a state of denial about the problem and they are unable to ascribe it to anything more specific than "stress." Jon is worried that he cannot, as a relatively well-educated layperson in the realm of therapy, really say much more about the girl's treatment. Should Jon stay out of the picture now, or continue to push along what he believes is the right path? When does Jon trust his instinct and judgments and when does Jon relax in the face of other realities?

Discussion Questions

1. What responsibilities does the school head have for student out-of-school problems? Where does the head's primary loyalty lie?

With the student? with the student's parents? The school? Oneself?
2. What would you do in this situation? Why?

HOW TO HANDLE A STUDENT'S INSENSITIVITY?

Ms. Williams turned her back during her 3rd-grade class to help a child with a homework question. She overheard John say to another child, "Fred can't even figure out what four plus four is. He had to use his fingers." Fred heard this comment and, on impulse, pushed the child down. John was upset and startled by Fred's impulsive behavior.

Ms. Williams told John to apologize to Fred for what he had said, but Fred was extremely agitated. He shouted, "Nobody likes me. They think I'm stupid." These impulsive outbursts were not uncommon to Fred; as the year progressed, they became more frequent and uncontrollable.

Ms. Williams was frustrated. She didn't know how to manage Fred's behavior and learning issues while still maintaining a productive learning environment for the other students in her class.

Fred had been struggling all year. His skills were poor in most subject areas, and he could see that he was well behind his peers, which frustrated him greatly. At first his peers tried to be supportive, but they soon became discouraged because Fred worked so slowly and often became angry when they tried to correct his mistakes. As a result, Fred alienated himself from the rest of the class.

Ms. Williams tried her best to tailor her lesson plans to meet Fred's needs. She would often spend instructional time working one-on-one with Fred, but this closer interaction proved unsuccessful. She began to see that the others in the class were suffering.

Fred's outbursts eventually became more physical, disrupting the class and creating a tense environment. Many parents had called Ms. Williams to complain, so she met with her director to discuss the situation. They agreed to call a meeting with Fred's parents and recommend that he be tested.

Fred's parents seemed to be pleased with the school's educational and administrative policies. They had one child in 5th grade who had been in the school for 5 years and was doing extremely well, and another in kindergarten who seemed to make the transition from preschool to kindergarten very easily.

At the meeting, Fred's parents, Mr. and Mrs. Daily, seemed to be receptive to Ms. Williams's recommendation about testing. They scheduled an appointment for Fred, and the results showed that Fred suffered from Attention Deficit Disorder and had some serious processing problems. Recommendations included intensive tutoring and therapy, which might lead to medication. The Dailys started with these processes but stopped therapy with two different doctors after each recommended medication as a partial solution.

Fred's behavior improved slightly, but the outbursts were still a daily threat. Once again the school administration, Ms. Williams, and the Dailys met. The school recommended that Fred's parents consider transferring him to another school, one that was more capable of dealing with his learning issues, but Mr. and Mrs. Daily insisted Fred stay in the school.

After much consideration, the school decided that it was in the best interest of all involved that Fred should be counseled out and that the school would deal with the Dailys' reaction, whatever that may be.

Discussion Questions

1.   Has the school reached a proper and just decision? If not, for which concerned parties is the decision unjust?
2.   How much responsibility should fall on the teacher in a case such as this?
3.   How can a selective school deal with students who are on vastly different learning paths than other students? Can the school ethically meet the needs of all kinds of students?

THE SCHOOL AS PARENT

Daniella Piazza was an elementary school teacher at a small suburban private school. She had been teaching 3rd grade for 4 years and she was just beginning to feel comfortable in her role. She loved the children she taught and had no trouble finding good and likeable qualities in them.

Daniella, however, was having considerable difficulty with one particular student. She found liking Hannah difficult: even though Hannah loved school and was a solid student, her behavior frustrated Daniella. Hannah rarely followed instructions, and she constantly tried to be the center of attention. She made faces in class, lifted her dress, or talked in a loud voice about her "boyfriend." She regularly disrupted her classmates' presentations. Daniella felt terrible that Hannah's behavior often got the whole class in trouble, but she didn't know what to do. It had become clear that punishing Hannah did not work, but the angry responses of Hannah's peers demanded attention.

Ms. Piazza had had many conferences with the parents, but it became clear that the parents did not want to focus on their daughter's negative behavior. Instead they chose to spend most of the conferences complaining about the work they had to put into raising Hannah and her siblings. The parents, who both worked long hours, said they expected the school to help them solve Hannah's behavioral problems.

Ms. Piazza began to realize that Hannah received very little attention from her parents and other adults. Hannah seemed lonely and sad, and she could roust herself from these doldrums only by making herself the center of attention.

Other clues to Hannah's home life worried Daniella more. Hannah began writing stories in her journal about the many pets that had died in Hannah's care. Ms. Piazza spoke to Hannah about her writing and Hannah admitted that she liked her pets' company but that she did not know how to take care of them.

Daniella felt at a loss as to how to help this child. Hannah's behavior was disruptive to the whole class, and Hannah was clearly unhappy. Ms. Piazza felt that without the cooperation of the parents the school would not be able to help Hannah, and the parents' cooperation seemed unlikely. Ms. Piazza struggled with whether she and the administration should counsel the child out of the school. She had seen how angry the parents had been with Hannah at the conferences, and she did not want to remove the positive and consistent influences of the school from Hannah's life.

Discussion Questions

1. Is physical abuse worse than neglect? Is there ever a time when neglect should be reported to child welfare?
2. Would the school be helping Hannah by counseling her out? In this case, which should take precedence: the school's interests, or Hannah's?
3. Many independent school parents demand that schools serve as much more than educational institutions. How much should the school be willing to get involved in personal and family issues and parenting styles? When, if ever, should the school try to force its opinions on the parent? At what point do parental demands for caretaking become unreasonable?

Illustration by Audrey Manning, Grade 9

7

Heads/Trustees/School Cases

At independent schools, paralleling the public school's board of education, there is a board of trustees. Paralleling the public school superintendents and principals, there are independent school heads, principals, division directors, and deans. All those who fill these positions are charged with taking a broad view of the well-being of the school as a whole. Even though there is a hierarchical structure here, each level shares the same basic goal. But the good of the school can be viewed differently by each of these different entities. Moreover, they each also can act in ways that can be ethically questionable, and others in the school population may question their leadership.

The cases in this chapter display situations that raise ethical dilemmas about a board member making a special request for his child's placement to a school head, the fairness of a school head closing down all the student computers as punishment for a few hackers' abuse of the system, a school newspaper stretching the boundaries of free expression, an administrator finding a packet of drugs on a school trip, a board chair and school head experiencing friction in their roles, a school head firing a secretary, and a school head confronting the board with a case of their possible conflict of interest.

HEAD AND TRUSTEE WITH TEACHER IN THE MIDDLE

Village Academy is a pre-kindergarten through 8th grade coeducational day school of approximately 200 students. Halstead Smithers had been a member of the board for 4 years, and board chair for 3. Susan Walker was in her 2nd year as head of school, having come to headship from her role as a divisional director. Susan and Halstead had an excellent relationship: friendly, open, and mutually supportive. Susan was particularly impressed with Halstead's ability to coolly analyze situations and with his clear sense of the proper role of board and administration.

Improving attrition and retention was one of the key goals that Susan and the board had placed high on their annual agenda. While the focus of these efforts primarily involved narrowing the range of students that the school could realistically serve in the lower school, there was a lingering impression among some parents that the middle-school curriculum could be strengthened. Susan and Halstead both agreed that applications to other independent schools were still too common at the upper grades.

As Halstead and Susan finished their weekly appointment one November day, the conversation turned to Halstead's daughters, Sarah and Margaret. Sarah, an 8th grader, was in the process of her high school applications. Halstead and his wife were pleased with Sarah's experience at the school, but they had ongoing concerns about the capabilities of Jane Parker, the 6th-grade homeroom teacher. They felt that Ms. Parker's weaknesses as a teacher had hurt Sarah's academic development, particularly in math. Of course, as parents of a daughter, this was of particular concern to them. Mrs. Smithers felt particularly strongly about Ms. Parker's fundamental inadequacy as a teacher. Indeed, Halstead said, they would be withdrawing their younger daughter, Margaret, a rising 6th grader, if Ms. Parker were to continue as the 6th-grade teacher for the following year.

Susan and Halstead had ongoing discussions about the faculty evaluation process and about the fact that in Susan's opinion, there were no grounds for dismissing Ms. Parker. While there were areas to strengthen in her teaching, these were well within the range of professional goals that any teacher might need to improve upon. Changing Ms. Parker's teaching assignment would also be problematic. Ms. Parker was committed to 6th grade and enjoyed it a great deal. As a small school with one section per grade, moving Ms. Parker would require moving another teacher into 6th grade. Currently, there was not a candidate for such a move. In addition, it would require an explanation for the move. Conceding to parental pressure under threat of a student's withdrawal seemed a slippery slope.

Halstead understood each of these arguments. He emphasized the importance of communicating the evaluation system to parents, including his wife. He respected the school's right to make any and all evaluative judgments about a teacher's competence. However, he felt that his wife was intractable on the issue, and applications would, indeed, move forward. Sensitive to the impact of the board chair withdrawing a child, he stated that his elder daughter's graduation provided a good reason for his family to "move the girls together" and that this would be the only public explanation given for Margaret's premature departure from the school. But Susan knew that the real reason could not be hidden for long. She also knew that no matter how understanding the board chair was, she still had to work with him, and things would be different from now on.

Discussion Questions

1. For the good of long-term relations with the board chair, should Susan reconsider? If yes, on what grounds? If no, why not?
2. Should Susan try to ease Ms. Parker out? Would that be ethical?

EVOLVING COMPUTER ETHICS

The academic world still struggles with the ethics of print media. Plagiarism occurs on every secondary school or university campus every year, and the defense is frequently mounted that the accused did not understand the proper protocol for citations. Given this continuing challenge in the print media, it is small wonder that we are just beginning to sort out academic standards for the electronic media, where access to a universe of content seems almost unlimited and "cut and paste" is a simple command with a click of a mouse. (This is my story as a school head of one incident that reflects the complications that can arise in the new world of electronic media.)

In the early 1990s, before the explosion of access to the Internet, we had a robust local area network at the Eaton School. All students and faulty had e-mail accounts and access to the network. Forums were common additions to classroom discussions, papers were routinely word-processed and often presented in multimedia format on a disk, and the network evolved in ways we could not have imagined to become a kind of nervous system for the academic set. We did anticipate that questions of academic honesty would arise, and before students received access, they were required to read and sign a contract that outlined expectations for behavior on our network. No downloading or insertion of programs without permission, no profanity or insulting remarks directed toward individuals or groups, no invasion of the account of another person, and careful crediting of the work of others were keystones in the contract.

Early in January network administrators began alerting academic administrators that there was a growing amount of violation of this contract. Accounts were entered without authorization, work was deleted or altered, and minor viruses were introduced that left "humorous" messages in unexpected places. The group pondered these actions and alternative responses for some time, considering and then rejecting a number of proposals.

One option considered was to purchase higher-level security programs to preclude the unauthorized entry of accounts. The problem with that was that it simply increased the stakes and made the mischief more of a game. All of us were certain that eventually the students could foil any security software we installed. Why give them the satisfaction of escalating their tricks of avoidance of security measures to circumvent increasingly sophisticated protection software?

We could supervise all hardware more closely, perhaps locking every room with a computer if an adult supervisor was not present. The problem with this response was that it violated our basic principle of maximum access, would probably fail within the school because of consistent implementation in a setting where almost every room had a computer, and would certainly fail with external entry into our system through the telephone lines.

We could track the electronic trail of the mischief-makers and catch them in the act. The problem with this was that we knew that a skilled hacker could disguise himself as another person on the system, so that although we could have strong suspicions we were not likely to have the certainty necessary to impose serious sanctions. In addition, this approach would not seize the "teachable moment" for the entire community, as it would be a relatively invisible transaction with a substantial probability of promoting the hackers to the status of heroes for the principle of privacy and First Amendment rights.

One of the interesting aspects of our consideration of all these alternatives was that although we held several meetings in which all of the technical staff and all of the educational administrators discussed various approaches, for the most part this "conversation" was carried on online. Although we were using an administrative forum that had special security provisions, we all realized that our culprits could easily have penetrated this barrier and could be reading over our shoulders our exchanges, laughing at our primitive ability to maintain order in hyperspace.

President's Day weekend, a 3-day holiday, was rapidly approaching when we decided on the approach that we would take to address this problem. On Friday, just at the end of school, we alerted all faculty members to the fact that the network would be closed when everyone returned to school the following Tuesday morning, and that teachers should plan their work accordingly. We then took a risk and called in the editors of the student newspaper, *The Eatonian,* and, swearing them to secrecy, told them that on Tuesday morning the students, upon entering the building, would confront stern faced administrators who would herd all students and teachers into an emergency assembly. At the assembly the headmaster would outline the violations, and announce that the network would be closed immediately and remain closed until the culprits came forward to acknowledge their own culpability. Students would be told that we did not desire any reporting by student or teacher of any actions done by others; we wanted self-reporting. We announced that sanctions would definitely be imposed, but that they would be less serious if students acknowledged their crimes than if we had to catch the hackers through an electronic trail. Finally, we suggested that anyone skilled enough to indulge in this mischief knew that they were creating an electronic trail and that, therefore, we had a very good fix on the identity of those involved. We could not wait long for the individuals to step forward to acknowledge their crimes. This gave the student newspaper a rare opportunity to actually print real news. Without violating our confidence, over the weekend they set about producing a special issue to be handed to all students as they left the assembly, including the text of the head's remarks at that assembly and some editorial response to those remarks: the definition of a scoop.

The reaction to the announcement in the assembly was predicable: "You cannot do that—I have a paper due today that is on the system. It is not fair to punish all of us for the sins of a few! This is destroying the school. . . . It is a violation of our honor system!" The adult response was also predictable. Because they were informed about the action in advance and endorsed this approach, all faculty members gave similar supportive responses without questioning its justice. Of course, we responded with more confidence than we really felt, since we were not certain that the culprits would confess and we did not know how long, in fact, we wished to keep the system closed.

Discussion Questions

1. Is it right to punish all students for the transgressions of a few? Was there any other alternative?
2. Given the ubiquity of computers in the schools, how should "netiquette" be taught and ethical codes for the proper use of cyberspace be developed? Does this require a new ethics, or can time-honored and in-place ethical principles do the job?

STUDENT NEWSPAPERS:
FREE SPEECH AND ADMINISTRATIVE RESPONSIBILITY

Dan Dryden was the new director of the high school at an independent pre-K–12 school located in the suburbs of a large city. Knowing that the school emphasized writing and, in fact, produced an excellent literary magazine each year, he was eager to revive the school newspaper, which had become inactive because of a lack of student interest. Fortunately, he soon found a senior, Adam, who was eager to take on the responsibilities of editing the paper and a teacher who was willing to advise it. Dan had no particular agenda for the newspaper and, indeed, believed that the students who wrote and produced it should shape its mission and editorial policy, and even determine what to call it. In this, he believed that he was consistent with the school's mission, which emphasized that its pedagogy was "child-centered" and "experiential."

The only guideline that Dan asked Adam to follow was to develop a code of conduct to which the staff of the newspaper would adhere. He suggested that this code of conduct include a provision that no articles contain anything that would slander or offend a member of the school community. Adam agreed, but made it clear to both Dan and the faculty adviser that he felt the adviser's role should be limited to providing editorial advice when the staff asked for it, and reminding them of their code of conduct when he felt an article threatened to violate it. Other than this, his role was expected to be hands-off. Dan and the adviser assented to this request, believing that it would build trust with the editor and his staff, as well as providing the most productive context in which the staff could learn from their own mistakes.

Adam soon assembled his staff, developed a code of conduct along the lines that Dan had suggested, and wrote a mission statement that eloquently stressed the need for the paper to reflect the racial and cultural diversity of the school community. In order to symbolize this diversity, Adam wanted to print the newspaper on brightly colored paper and, in fact, call it *The Colored Paper*. While Dan and the advisor admired the inclusive ethos Adam and his staff hoped the paper would embody, they were concerned that the negative connotations of the word "colored" would undermine the paper's intentions. They pointed out to Adam the notorious role this word had played in the history of race relations in the United States and South Africa, and expressed their anxiety that some members of the school community, and especially people of color, might be offended. Further, Dan asked

Adam to consider whether or not the name violated the code of conduct that Adam had just formulated. Then he suggested that Adam might want to change the name of the paper to something that still conveyed the theme of diversity, but was not racially loaded. Adam said that he appreciated Dan's concern, and would discuss it with his staff and then get back to him.

The next day, Adam told Dan that he and his staff felt strongly about keeping the name *The Colored Paper*. They did not think that it was as controversial as Dan did. If it did upset some people, they hoped to use it as an opportunity to "raise consciousness" about issues of diversity. Dan tried one final time to persuade Adam to change the name but, cautious of interfering too much and micromanaging what he strongly believed should be a student-run enterprise, he said, "I don't agree with your decision, but I respect it" and hoped that whatever fallout occurred would provide teachable moments from which Adam and his staff could benefit. But he still felt trepidation, which only intensified over the next couple of weeks as the publication of the first issue drew nearer.

It did not take long after the paper was distributed for Dan to realize the worst of his fears. Although Adam had printed his eloquent mission statement prominently on the front page and the paper contained several articles by students of color, these were evidently overshadowed in some people's minds by the paper's masthead. Several parents called Dan with accusations that ranged from being too permissive to, as one especially angry parent said, "perpetuating institutional racism." Even though Dan had anticipated these complaints, it was painful for him to hear them. He listened as patiently as he could and urged parents to look beyond what the paper was called to the positive ways in which the contents reflected its admirable, if idealistic, mission. Privately, he agonized over whether he should have acted more forcefully with Adam and his staff and insisted that they change the name of the paper. Should he have stressed the importance of social responsibility over freedom of expression? But wasn't Adam acting in a socially responsible way by giving the paper a multicultural focus? Moreover, hadn't Dan himself acted responsibly by protecting their freedom of expression?

The paper had a decidedly different impact on the students than it had on their parents. Their concern was not what the paper was called, but what they regarded as the "preachy" tone of some of the articles. Not surprisingly, Adam was more nervous about his peers' criticism than the strong objections Dan told him he had received from some of the parents. Still, Adam agreed to discuss changing the name with his staff. When the next issue came out a few weeks later, it was still printed on colored paper. But its masthead read *The Palette.*

Discussion Questions

1. The balance, and often conflict, between social responsibility and freedom of expression is one with which newspapers and other media have struggled. Given the particular circumstances of this conflict at Dan's school, how can "social responsibility" be defined? What was the most socially responsible action that a) Dan and b) Adam could have taken? Similarly, how can "freedom of expression" be defined? If Dan had insisted that Adam change the name of the paper, how would he have limited Adam and his staff's freedom to express themselves?
2. Had you been in Dan's place, what would you have done and why? How would you have used this situation to teach Adam within the student-centered and experiential pedagogy and culture of Adam's school?

WHAT IS THIS STUFF?

The first day of the ski trip had gone quite well, and the bus was loaded for the trip back to the mountain for day two, when a chaperone from the tour company and the tour operator asked to see Mr. Malcolm, the director of the upper school. The chaperone had found something in a room, something that he was sure was not good news.

Mr. Malcolm accompanied the chaperone and the tour operator to a room in the lodge where the chaperone pointed out a Baggie he had found that contained a brown-gray substance he simply did not recognize.

Mr. Malcolm asked, "What is this stuff?"

"Hash, some sort of poor, street-quality hash," came the reply.

"Are you sure?"

"Yes, I'm sure that's what I'm looking at," said the chaperone.

Mr. Malcolm turned to the tour operator and asked, "Harold, what do you think it is?"

"I'm not so sure. It could be what he says it is, but I don't know."

Thoughts raced through Mr. Malcolm's head: he had worried about a few students on the trip during the year, and he was even worried that they didn't look quite right when they got on the bus yesterday at the end of a long day of skiing. In fact, if he had had to bet, he would have put a couple of bucks on their having been stoned. But he hadn't seen them smoking, and he had not yet ever searched a student or his possessions.

On the previous day, however, Mr. Malcolm had been concerned enough to ask Harold, the veteran charter trip operator, to have a close look at the kids Mr. Malcolm was worried about, and talk to them if he also was suspicious. The tour operator, who sees kids on such trips week after week, spoke to the boys, but didn't perceive anything that worried him. Of course, Mr. Malcolm wondered: I see them every day, and I know what they look like and act like all the time, so maybe I'm the one whose hunch is right. But having asked someone else to check on it, he dropped the matter.

So the following day, when another chaperone found and identi-fied this stuff, his worry appeared to be confirmed. But what should he do now? He had a sense that at least one of the guys in that room was a risk as a pot smoker. The chaperone was sure this was hash. Mr. Malcolm didn't know what he was looking at. The group had a full day on the slopes and a long ride home left to go. Standing in the bright sunshine in the parking lot, Mr. Malcolm had to make a decision.

Discussion Questions

1. Mr. Malcolm hadn't yet spoken to the students in question. How should he approach them? He had a very strong opinion from someone he had no reason to doubt, and he had his own suspi-cions and concerns, in particular about one of the students he needed to question. Should he trust his instincts and what he had been told? How should he proceed?
2. There was a chance, of course, that students on the trip had brought drugs or alcohol along, even if what was in the Baggie was not a drug. Balancing the right to privacy with protecting the safety and well-being of the students, as well as the integrity of the trip and school rules, might mean Mr. Malcolm should search the students and their belongings. Does Mr. Malcolm have the right to do so?
3. Assuming that the student who acknowledges the substance denies that it is an illegal drug (and he does), how does Mr. Malcolm handle the situation? Does he drop it? Whom does he call? Does the student get to ski? What does he say to the head of the school? To the parents?

A MISTRUSTFUL TRUSTEE

After a long and hard year of school, John Bradley, the head of the Brookline School in urban Tempest City, finally settled down for a month of rest, reflection, and a real August vacation. This had been the most exhausting, draining, and difficult year he had ever had in more than 20 years as a school head. Nevertheless, he was happy—he now has a new board chair whom he fully supports and several new administrators who are eager to test their abilities and show great promise. So, he wonders why he is still pensive, somewhat depressed, and unsettled. Perhaps it is because there had been no real closure with the departing board president, Sandra Cranberry, and the more he thinks about the situation with Ms. Cranberry, the more confused he becomes about the professional ethics of the situation that unfolded.

Hard-working, dedicated, and committed to the Brookline School, Ms. Cranberry took on the board presidency several years ago with enthusiasm. An efficient and effective business professional, she was goal-oriented, and made sure that each and every board member fulfilled their fiduciary responsibilities through time, work, and resources. She was a meticulous perfectionist, and made sure that every written agenda for a committee or board meeting was faxed to her for at least one proofreading even after it was reviewed by John.

During the first two or three years Sandra and John developed a very cordial relationship, and established the necessary partnership between board chair and head. Together they led and managed the board, accomplishing the completion of an ambitious and much-needed capital campaign drive to benefit the school's endowment. It quickly became of concern to John, however, that Sandra often became involved in issues that were not the business of the board chair. For instance, she would complain to John about the way that the professional staff members of the Institutional Advancement Office dressed: often not in business suits but in more casual attire. John was amazed when Sandra made this comment, but did not know how to argue the point. John believed that the staff members dressed appropriately, as they always looked neat and professional. After the incident, John became more conscious of his own appearance and made sure that his attire was always appropriate for weekly meetings with Sandra.

As time passed, John became increasingly uptight and overly cautious when meeting with his board chair. Sandra was becoming too involved in issues that were not within her area of responsibility. When hiring new administrators, John would report to Sandra about the process and his choice of candidates, and often Sandra would object and make a comment like "I hope that you know what you are doing." Over time, it became apparent that Sandra could not keep herself out of the day-to-day business of the school, and she often put John in a difficult position.

John mentioned to Sandra that in the new fiscal year he would like to see a rotation of some committee chairs, particularly in the fund-raising committee. Sandra did not agree, and said that she thought the chair was doing an excellent job. After several months of discussion, John learned that the fund-raising committee chair was a good friend of Sandra's, and so Sandra was reluctant to jeopardize their relationship. Even after John convinced Sandra that a change had to be made, Sandra wanted John to talk to the chair. John did not think that it was his responsibility to admonish a board member or to unseat a committee chair, and so once again began to believe that Sandra was not supporting his work.

John reflected on the early days of his relationship with Sandra, when he wanted Sandra to be the board chair even though he knew she was a very demanding and difficult trustee. At the time John thought that Sandra was the best candidate for the job, as she was a savvy, intelligent, ambitious go-getter. John thought that he and Sandra would be able to lead the board to be best it could be, and that he could rise above any criticism and be able to deal with Sandra's demands. Had he been wrong?

In the last year with Sandra as board chair, John very much wanted to maintain a good relationship. He needed a positive relationship with the exiting chair and wanted approval of his work as head. Instead, John began to feel that Sandra was becoming involved in even more issues that were not in the domain of her responsibilities. He felt increasingly alienated by Sandra, a feeling exacerbated when Sandra told John not to come to the board retreat, as the board could "talk more freely about many issues without the head present." Sandra said she would report the details to John, and so John agreed. Normally the school head participates in the board retreat unless he or she has been dismissed or has resigned for the coming year. After the retreat, Sandra, who was usually so prompt with phone calls, did not call John for nearly two weeks, nor did she share the results of the board questionnaire with him. In addition, the facilitator of the board retreat neglected to contact John and brief him about what went on or share the results of the questionnaire. John realized that he was not imagining the difficulties in his relationship with Sandra. He decided to take a new direction—to be more assertive and open about his thoughts and ideas than he used to be.

John confronted the facilitator about failing to report on the retreat, and worked assiduously to let the board know that the process was wrong. He also worked very hard to support a candidate whom he very much wanted as the next board chair, despite Sandra's strong opposition. Sandra considered Natalie, the candidate, to possess no real leadership potential, but John felt differently. John believed that while Natalie had no board leadership experience, she was as savvy and intelligent as Sandra and had the potential to be very successful. When discussing the future leadership of the board, John said that Natalie would be the best choice, and Sandra became irritated and upset, making the comment, "You want a board chair who will do things your way." Needless to say, John was not surprised by this comment.

After several months of hard work and incredible politicking by the Nominating Committee, Natalie was voted in as board chair. At the end-of-year board party there were many good feelings as the retiring trustees were applauded with citations for their devoted service to the board. Here, of course, Sandra was the star, and John made the appropriate complimentary remarks about her outstanding service to the school. As he made those comments, however, he could not help but have a feeling of relief. His lack of sincere feelings of regret at Sandra's departure made him feel guilty. Sandra rounded out the evening by complimenting John on his outstanding work as school head, so no one ever really knew what had gone on between them.

As he looked back at the year, John realized that he had never felt so lonely in his role as a school head and that he will need some time to think about his relationship with the new board chair. What will Natalie be like? What will be her hidden agenda? In a disagreement about an issue, how will Natalie react? How will John react? Will it be seen as a power struggle? Can they talk honestly and dispute differences for the sake of the school and feel good about the outcome? John is determined to bring about Natalie's success as board chair. What can John do to facilitate Natalie's success? He feels that he has lots of thinking to do so that the new school year will unfold smoothly and successfully.

Discussion Questions

1. Is this a case about ethics? Power? Professional behavior?
2. In contemporary ethics, the ethics of caring and of relationship has challenged the more traditional ethics of principle and duty, making ethics a more personal engagement with others. Could

this be a case of being morally right in principle but morally wrong in relationship?
3. How could John avoid similar problems in his relationship with future board chairs?

A LOYAL EMPLOYEE

Rita believes that all of us, particularly those of us who work in schools, should be mindful of the need to be respectful of persons at all ages along a broad spectrum. From the youngest child to the most elderly adult in our school community, we should strive to practice and model the qualities of respect, cooperation, honesty, and hard work. Little did Rita know, however, that in trying to practice these virtues, she would become embroiled in an ethical dilemma personally and professionally.

Several years ago, long before the sensitivity expected with the passage of ADA laws and regulations, Rita was interviewing candidates for the position of school secretary. After doing numerous interviews with a range of applicants from those just out of high school and secretarial school to former CEO's secretaries, the person who emerged as the most qualified candidate was a woman in her early sixties who was recently widowed and, having just moved to California, wanted to work another three or four years. Betty had worked as a school secretary in a large public school, had begun her secretarial career as a legal secretary, and had wonderful skills.

Rita hired Betty with no concern about her age and began what was to become a long and very cordial personal and professional relationship. Over time, the school hired additional clerical help and Betty worked more and more closely with Rita, doing much of the correspondence for her office as head of school. What was originally intended to be 3 or 4 years turned to 5, then 10 and more. After working for the school for more than 10 years, Betty's health began to fail. Increasingly, Betty became troubled with a bad back, arthritis, and a digestive disorder, and had a series of surgeries, including cancer surgery and back surgery. She suffered from high blood pressure, and as she grew older, she began to have periods of light-headedness and dizziness. Three times she passed out at school and was found unconscious on the floor of the bathroom and another time in the school garage. On at least two occasions the paramedics were called to respond to incidents that occurred during the workday.

Increasingly working in pain, Betty became less than patient and more irritable with co-workers. The bending and lifting that were required to file was beyond her physically. The bulk mailings she was assigned that needed to be run off and collated were delegated to others rather than handled. The office supplies that needed to be unpacked, inventoried, and put away could no longer be done. She was the staff member who worked in closest proximity to the infirmary, and it became evident that she could no longer be expected to keep an eye on children when one day she turned off the lights on a sleeping child and left for the day. As the school grew and the demands on the office accelerated and became more complex, Rita was urged by the board to hire a secretary just for herself.

By this time, Betty was in her early seventies and Rita began to have conversations about Betty taking more time off and enjoying her retirement. With each conversation and each evaluation, Betty became increasingly defensive and said that she would never retire. It became obvious shortly after her 75th birthday that the school needed to make some changes, despite the obvious fondness for her as a person.

Having moved Betty several years earlier to a windowless back office by the infirmary over her protests, Rita went to her and suggested that she change her office space to one in the front reception area where she could see and be seen by more of the school community. Rita had also gotten permission from the board to cut back Betty's work schedule and offer her fewer days but at the same salary. It was believed that if Betty had more time at home and began to enjoy it, she might consider retirement as an alternative that was more attractive. Knowing that money was not an issue for her made it easier for Rita to contemplate these changes.

When Rita called Betty in and told Betty that she was going to be hiring a new position as secretary to the head of school and that she was asking Betty to change work spaces and an altered work schedule at the same pay, Betty was furious. Betty felt that she was being demoted and not rewarded for her years of service to the school. Further, she felt that the only reason we were contemplating these changes was because of her age. Despite having had conversations over time about her increasing inability to do many of the things on her job description and the accommodations we had made for her, Betty felt humiliated. Her response was to shut her office door and refuse to speak to Rita about the contemplated changes. She also stated unequivocally that she would not move to another space in the offices.

What ensued was a week of teary conversations, discussions of alternatives, and hostile silences. Finally, at the end of that week, Rita had to give Betty a choice: either Betty moved after the weekend to the new work space and accepted the conditions as outlined, or Rita would have to ask that Betty submit her resignation and not return to work. Monday morning, she did not return, did not call, and did not respond to Rita's calls. By Wednesday, Rita wrote and asked that Betty offer an explanation for her absence or return to work. At the end of that week, the School received a letter from Betty's lawyer with language alluding to age discrimination, constructive discharge, and so forth.

Discussion Questions

1. Although this case ends on a legal note, our concern here is not with legality, but with ethical behavior. Do you think Rita acted ethically? Do you think Betty acted ethically?
2. Could this situation have been handled differently so that a loyal employee could leave the institution with her head held high rather than disappearing from the school community without farewells or celebration?

A FAIRY TALE?

The Regents School was in very severe financial difficulty, essentially insolvent in a technical sense, unable to pay its cumulative deficit of over half a million dollars and unable to borrow money to make up for the shortfall in the operating budget for the coming year. With a severe reduction in enrollment at the grammar school level, the board already had voted to place the five brownstones housing the lower school up for sale with the hope that the Regents School could get out of debt and maintain a healthy, ongoing 7–12 upper school. While Peter, the new school head, did not like the plan to close the lower school before he had been given a chance to work on its problems, he recognized the school's severe financial circumstances, and supported and participated in the effort to sell the brownstones for $3.5 million.

However, Peter discovered a week or so before a board meeting in the early spring of his first year that a member of the board, with the concurrence and knowledge of the chairman of the board, had negotiated with a prominent real estate firm to receive a commission on the sale of the five brownstones. When Peter discovered the conflict of interest involved in the potential sale, namely that a trustee would directly benefit financially, he challenged the arrangement at a private meeting with the Executive Committee. The Executive Committee essentially told Peter to "play ball" or else. Faced with that dilemma, Peter resolved to confront the entire board with the situation, although Peter assumed that given the longstanding tenure of the Executive Committee (the board president, for example, had been in his position for over 15 years) he would be patted on the back for his nearly 1 year of service and offered good wishes for his next position—elsewhere!

Shortly thereafter, Peter met with the board of trustees and made clear his position on the ethical dilemma/conflict of interest issue. He also told them that he thought Regents needed new leadership on the board, and that he would indeed continue as head only on one condition, namely that the entire executive committee resign and be replaced by an executive committee of his choice. He also talked about the necessity of having new leadership and moving the school forward in a variety of ways, from fund-raising to helping create a new sense of confidence among the larger school community, and ended by saying that he would sit outside the boardroom and await their decision. He fully expected the board to support the executive committee and maintain the status quo. But after 45 minutes or so, the door opened and Peter was greeted not with a good-bye, but with applause. The Executive Committee agreed to resign at the end of the year, to be replaced by new leadership of Peter's choice, both from the board and ultimately from new board members. This was all accompanied by the offer of a 5-year contract and a commitment to support Peter in his plans for the school's future. Today, Regents School is, fortunately, one of the most successful schools in Manhattan.

Granted, this is a fairy-tale ending, but it is based on a true incident. Nevertheless, there is room for some questions.

Discussion Questions

1. Why does the triumph of principled behavior seem to stretch the imagination in today's world?
2. Was the trustee receiving the commission unethical or helping the school by using his influence to facilitate the sale?
3. Was Peter foolhardy and lucky or brave and deserving?
4. If the outcome had been different, what difference, if any, might there have been for the future of Regents School or for Peter's career?

APPENDIX A

Student Understandings of Right and Wrong

This appendix contains a substantial representation of how students from various age groups (pre-K–12th grade) understand right and wrong. The following sample of student writing is from an annual All School Write-In during one of the years in which Ethics was a schoolwide theme. On this particular morning teachers in all grades stopped their activities at a certain time and read aloud the following instructions: "This morning the entire school, from pre-K through 12th grade, is participating in the thirteenth annual All School Write-In. You will have fifty minutes to compose an essay on how do you know what is right from what is wrong. Describe a situation where you acted on what you knew was right when it took courage for you to do so. Before you begin to write you should first take some time to gather and organize your thoughts. You may wish to jot down some notes, make an outline or write a rough draft. Please do your best to express your ideas clearly." In the pre-K and first grade classes the children dictated their sentences or words to their teachers. A few weeks after the All School Write-In, selected essays were shared at an assembly for the entire school.

We hope that looking at these essays and seeing the progression of the understanding of right and wrong from pre-K through 12th grade will help our readers appreciate what developmental psychologists like Piaget, Kohlberg, Gilligan, and others. have told us about the paths and forms that moral development takes in children's lives. References to some of their theoretical work appear in the Suggested Readings section, but here we can see the raw data: the responses of children to queries about their conception of right and wrong. These responses provide great insight into their developing perception and their range of sophistication with respect to the moral sphere. We hope that this information will provide educators with a reminder that the mind of a child is constantly forming and that each educator has the responsibility to nurture those minds not only intellectually, but morally.

PRE-K, KINDERGARTEN, AND LOWER SCHOOLS (GRADES 1–4)

Pre-K Class I

We read The Hole in the Dike *by Norma Green/Pictures by Eric Carle, a story about a young boy in Holland who saved his country from a flood by sticking his finger in the dike. We asked the children, "Tell us about a time when you did the right thing by helping someone." These were some of their responses:*

> My friend Dottie fell down and I helped her up.
> Sometimes my brother gets hurt because I hurt him and I say sorry
>   and he feels better.
> My brother's shoe was untied so I held him so he could tie it.
> My brother's finger got stuck and I helped him get it out.

Pre-K Class II

We asked the children, "How do you know what is right from what is wrong? Describe a situation in which you acted on what you knew right when it took courage for you to do so." These were some of their responses:

> If somebody punches your back, that's wrong.
> It's good to give somebody a toy if they want one.
> It's not good to kill a butterfly because then it won't
>   grow a new baby and it won't protect it.
> If someone pinches, it's wrong.

Kindergarten

How do you know when something's right or wrong?

> If someone tells you.
> In class, the teacher tells you what is wrong and what is right.
> When something's bad you have a time-out so you know it's bad.
> Someone will say "good boy/good girl."
> I just feel it, inside.
> When you're doing something that you're not supposed to, you get in
>   trouble, then you know it's wrong.
> You know it's right when you don't get time-out.
> When you hit someone on the head you know it's wrong because they cry.

> When you do something that makes someone feel better, that's
> right.
> When you share with someone, they are happy, that's a good thing, a
> right thing!
> When you hurt someone's feelings, it's wrong. They cry!
> Helping my friends is a right thing because it makes them feel good.
> When you bite someone, it's wrong. Because you hurt them and they
> cry. So you know it's a wrong thing to do.
> When you share with other people, they smile and you know they are
> happy and that's good, that's a right thing to do.
> If you keep a promise, that's a right thing. If you don't keep a promise,
> that's wrong because it makes you sad.
> When you tell a lie it's wrong because it makes people feel bad.

Elementary Grades

How do you know what is right from what is wrong? Describe a situation in which you acted on what you knew was right when it took courage for you to do so.

1ST GRADE
One time I told my neighbor that he had to stop smoking. It is hard to tell a grown-up what to do.

2ND GRADE
I went on a rocket. We traveled to the moon. The whole moon was made of gold. One man said, "Let's steal treasure from the gold moon." Should I be rich or do the right thing? I did the right thing. I didn't steal. I flew away in the escape capsule.

4TH GRADE
When you do something right you feel good inside, but if you did something wrong you wouldn't feel as good as you thought you'd feel. Once when I was little my dad said that I was good enough to have some friends over, so I did. Then when we were playing one of them said, "Why don't we sneak some cookies?" Of course, they all agreed to do this, except me. My dad had done me a favor and to thank him in return with stolen cookies was just not right. I was the only one who knew where they were. So it was my decision. First I thought about my friends, then my dad. Things raced through my mind: I would get in trouble. I might lose my friends. I would have a lie on my hands. Then, finally, I said, "But that would be wrong, and we could just ask," and did. I felt better!

MIDDLE SCHOOL (GRADES 5–8)

5TH GRADE

I think that you know what's right and wrong because you have been taught by your parents. When you were younger, maybe one or two years old, sometimes you'd tell your parents what you did at a friend's house. Sometimes your parents would be proud, other times they'd say "that's wrong." Over the years your parents kept telling you what's right and what's wrong. Every time your parents told you what was wrong, your mind noted it. As you grew up your mind filled up with right and wrong things. At the right age your parents maybe started to punish you for doing the wrong things. Not too serious at first, a time-out maybe; then maybe a grounding. You may get mad at your parents for punishing you but you must remember that it's hard for them to do the right thing.

Also, teachers influence you to do the right thing. They might send you to the office for bad behavior. You may think your teacher's being mean. Your teacher is actually helping you by teaching you right and wrong. What some people think is right, may be wrong for others. Slavery, for example, was right for the plantation owner, but wrong for the blacks. And when Abe Lincoln abolished slavery it was right for him, the north, and the blacks, but it was wrong for plantation owners who couldn't keep up the plantations without the extra help. Even the people who burn churches and write Nazi signs on Jewish graves must think that it was right at the time. If they were caught they'd go to jail, so it's wrong.

5TH GRADE

I know what is right and what is wrong because I get a funny feeling inside when something is wrong and I get a really good feeling when I'm right.

When I was walking home with my friend Jennifer and we were crossing a two way street, the sign said Don't Walk and no cars were coming. So Jennifer said, "Come on, Theresa, let's cross." I knew I wasn't supposed to cross against the light but then I remembered my dad and he said that he wanted me to come home in one piece. He also said don't take chances. Then I remembered my mom saying, "No matter how embarrassed you might be don't let anyone convince you that it is okay to cross against the light because it is not okay to get hit by a car." Then I knew how upset my parents would be if they ever found out that I did cross against the light after all those lectures they gave me. So I turned around to Jennifer and said, "No, it is not right to do that. You can go right ahead and cross and then I will meet you on the other side of the street when it says walk." So Jennifer said, "Okay, let's wait until it says walk." The pictures of my mom and dad in my head smiled and I knew I did the right thing.

6TH GRADE

The way you can tell right from wrong is that you look at your situation from three angles: Backwards, forwards, and inside-out. What I mean is look at your choice, right or wrong, from the "wrong" angle, the "right" angle, and then put yourself in someone else's position looking at your wrong or right choice. What do you think of yourself? If you look stupid or embarrassed, I suggest you not put yourself in that position. Billions of people do the right thing every ten seconds, yet only millions do the wrong thing every ten seconds. That's pretty good. We could work on it a little harder, though.

One time one of my friends was being really mean to me after we got in a fight. I got really mad because she was ganging up on me. A few days later I was still really mad. She asked me to help her in something. I didn't want to help her. Well, I helped her anyway. That's what friends do, not that I really wanted to be her friend just then, but I realized that friendship is a fragile thing, and if you drop it, you almost always break it. I think that I did the right thing because if I didn't help her, I would lose a friend. A friend can count for a thousand if she is a good friend.

Many people have done the right thing. Some have done wrong. I think that the hole of wrong doings can be patched. I know that people will try to patch it.

6TH GRADE

How do you know what is right or what is wrong?

Well first of all, you know that it's wrong if it is BAD like CHEATING or making people FEEL bad.

HAH! You know it's right if it's GOOD like being NICE or being a friend.

Once, I had a situation. Someone was writing swastikas in the bathroom. I knew who was DOing it. But I didn't want to tell my TEACHER 'cause the guy that was DOing it would BEAT ME UP!

So, I told my parents and they told my teacher and my teacher told my principal and my principal told Dr. Zubay and he got in trouble.

Then he beat me up. He also put a KNIFE to ME. But, I still GAINED courage and told on him. Now he's at POLY PREP. No more HIM!

A wrong thing is when YOUR friend steals something and you don't tell on him. TELL on him, find a new friend.

Bad and good
wrong and right
happy and sad . . .
DO THE RIGHT thing,
    be good and happy.

7TH GRADE

The horribly tough decision that stands out in my mind is from a long, long time ago. It's that devil-on-one shoulder and angel-on-the-other kind of situation. I was three or four years old and my biggest problem at the time was waiting for Saturday to come. During the week I just lazed around. It must have been in the early afternoon. My baby sitter was talking on the phone and I was in the kitchen. The plate of little cakes sat before me and I was tempted. My mom bought them for guests and she put them on a green plate. I must have stood for 15 minutes but in the end I left a full plate of pastries for a walk in the park.

7TH GRADE

I think how we determine if something is right or wrong is like a C++ program. When computers read a program, they go down through a list of things, like commands, places to type, et cetera, till they reach the end. The only "jumps" it makes are specifically put in, i.e., it cannot do things on its own. When determining whether something is right or wrong, your mind also goes through steps. Is it dangerous? against the rules? morals? The difference between computers and our brains is that we jump. Computer programs are completely linear, and while our minds are linear in general, we can jump from place to place.

I can't think of a time I have done something decidedly right in the face of wrong. However, without thinking about it, we do "right" things constantly. As Neanderthals, we would have been running around with axes killing each other. Now, we unconsciously follow rules. This is both a good and a bad thing. It makes us "civilized," but it also puts a cramp on creative thinking. You see, right and wrong are not clearly defined by computers, but they are defined by our jumpy minds.

8TH GRADE

I've known since I was a little kid, what's the difference between right and wrong. I know that stealing is wrong and being polite is right. However, sometimes situations become more complicated and the right thing to do is also the wrong thing to do. I know lying is wrong. However, if someone comes up to you and says, "Do you like my shirt?" and you think it is the most hideous thing you've ever seen, you shouldn't say that.

Sometimes situations become more serious. Once last year I was skating at P.S. 321, a public elementary school, with my friend and other kids. There was one kid there who was overweight and everyone was making fun of him. They were calling him names like "fatso" and other obnoxious names. Evan, my best friend, who didn't even know the kid, was pushing him down and screaming curses in his face. I don't really blame her though, because she was just following the crowd. I soon became really sick of all the name calling. So I told my friend to shut up.

A second later I turned around and I saw a bunch of the older kids jumping on top of the boy. They were wrestling with him and forcing him to lick the ground. Finally, I couldn't stand it. I knew that what they were doing was wrong, so I got up the courage and screamed at them to stop. Everyone turned around and stared at me. I was embarrassed, but I didn't care because I knew what they had been doing was wrong and I couldn't let it go on without saying anything. I told all of the boys who had been wrestling with the kid to leave him alone and to stop calling him names. I asked them how they would feel if someone was taunting them like that. Nobody said anything after that. Everyone just went off to somewhere else. I felt embarrassed and stupid, but I still felt good inside, because I had done the right thing. I got up the courage to stand up for what I believed in.

The way I figure out if something is right or wrong is, I try to imagine myself as the other person in the situation. If what I do makes that person upset then I know I have probably done the wrong thing.

Making the right decision is hard. Sometimes no matter what it takes, you have to stand up for what you believe is right, no matter what people think of you. In the end, you will feel more confident.

8TH GRADE

Many people ask you what they should do, and whether this choice is right or not, but the truth is that there is no real way to know right from wrong. Right and wrong are matters of opinion and morals. Almost everybody would say that stealing is wrong, but what if a poor man stole a loaf of bread so he and his family could eat dinner? Would that be wrong? Some people, including the poor man, would say it's right, but others would say it is wrong. I don't really know that answer. I'd probably say that the man was wrong with a justified reason. Then, from my point of view, whether something is wrong or right is taken to another degree, and then I ask the question of whether it is justifiable.

Once you decide if what you're doing is right or wrong, the next thing to do is the right thing. Some people do the wrong thing knowing that that it is wrong. It truly takes a lot of courage to do the right thing. I remember one incident which happened a few years back. My homeroom was like a family, with the exception of one kid. He was an outcast. Part of it was his fault because he was a pain, but the class was also at fault. He was the new kid, and had no friends in a strange new place. We, as the good people, should have made him feel welcome—that would've been the right thing to do. Instead we taunted him. Sometimes I felt like standing up for him because I thought it was the right thing to do, but I didn't because I wanted to be a part of the larger group. Now as I look back I wish I had had enough courage to stand up and do the right thing. In the end, we practically drove the kid right out of the school.

Knowing right from wrong is a matter of opinion and choosing right from wrong is a matter of choice.

8TH GRADE

Once I knew a girl named Jessica S. and she was 11 years old. She was a really good friend of mine the summer I was going into 6th grade. I could tell her anything and she could tell me anything. That summer she came over and we were spilling our guts to each other and she said, "Have you ever smoked?" I said, "No, of course not. Why? Have you?" She said, "Yeah, of course, with my 14 year-old boyfriend. He's the one who got me hooked on smoking but he does pot and I haven't tried that yet." I asked her why she did that and she said that it helped her lose weight (She was 190 lbs. at 11 years old) and she thought it was cool. I changed the subject but I still thought she was crazy.

A couple of weeks later this was still dwelling on me and I decided to do something about it. I called her mom and told her and now Jessica is not allowed to hang out with her ex-boyfriend and her mom doesn't trust her anymore. I felt bad after doing that and Jessica's not my friend any- more, but I felt it was the right thing to do. After all, I didn't want someone I cared about to get sick and ruin her health just to be so-called "cool" and there are other ways to lose weight.

UPPER SCHOOL (GRADES 9–12)

9TH GRADE

Right and wrong. It's a big issue. However, it isn't hard to figure out which one is which. My conscience tells me what I think is right and wrong. National laws tell me what is right and wrong. This isn't something that I necessarily have to dwell on.

I think that the way I have been brought up by my parents has given me good moral standards. I know when I have done something wrong. Because of this awareness I have I am able to feel guilty and tell someone the truth about what I have done.

There are no absolutes in right and wrong, everyone thinks differently depending on their personality. Just because I think something is wrong and I wouldn't ever do it, doesn't mean that someone else does.

For example, on the nationwide issue of guns, my dad and I think differ- ently. He thinks it's OK for people to have rifles for hunting, but I don't. I think it is wrong for anyone to have any sort of gun no matter what the circumstances.

It isn't whether or not I know what is right or wrong, it is what I think is right or wrong that is important. With so many people in this country from all over the world, everyone is bound to have different ideas. Nothing can change that. Why should anyone have to think like someone else anyway? People are naturally different so I think that it is right for people to think differently.

I can't think of an exact circumstance in which it has been hard for me to do the right thing. I either do the right thing or I don't. Sometimes what I think is right isn't in the long run and I pay for my mistake. So, you see right and wrong are totally up in the air. They can't be totally controlled, not even by our country's legal system.

These are touchy subjects that will never be agreed on by everyone.

9TH GRADE

Knowing the difference between right and wrong is based on a person's ethical knowledge. Basically, doing something right is something that is fair, that won't hurt you or anyone else. On the contrary, doing something wrong is something that will hurt you or anyone else in the long run, though it may seem like something fun or easy to do. One that does the right thing when they have the opportunity to do wrong is being courageous because others may oppose them and they are benefiting themselves by not taking the easy way out in a situation.

An example of when I had to choose right from wrong was when I was absent from school the day I had a big test in science. My friend told me that test was extremely easy and she would tell what exactly was on the test. At first I was going to take the information because I wasn't taking her answers or copying her during the test, so I didn't think that I would be cheating. Then I thought about the whole situation and I realized that it would be unfair to the other students to have the information about the test before I took it, while they didn't. Though others said I was doing a stupid thing and just to take the information, but I knew that I couldn't live with myself knowing that I cheated.

9TH GRADE

How do we know right from wrong? Why do shrinks have a job? I don't think that there is any formula or any equation to tell us the difference. I just think that we know the difference because it is our human nature.

I remember a long time ago, about five years, when I went to camp and was faced with the very same question. I had just finished playing baseball with friends and we were on our way to lunch. On the way we saw a wallet in the grass. Immediately my friends said let's see how much money there is in it. The second one of my friends said that a devil and an angel magically appeared on my shoulders. I guess my friends had the same two little people on their shoulders and we all had decided to return the wallet to the lost and found. I think that all of us were just too afraid to keep it because we might have gotten in trouble. Although it wasn't from the goodness of our hearts, we returned it.

If I were forced to give a reason why we know the difference between right and wrong, I would say because of fear.

9TH GRADE

I think most people don't know what is right and wrong. Some people say they do everything right, or everything wrong, but we all know that's not true. People can tell what is right and what is wrong by the feeling or the voice inside of them. To know what is right and what is wrong is a difficult thing to be able to deal with in life, but I think most people have a good conscience telling them which is best.

I know that I can tell what is wrong and right by the feelings and reactions I have in different situations. I would like to think that there is a devil on one side of my shoulder and an angel on the other, balancing out the good and the bad. I think I know the difference between right and wrong very well. If I feel scared, stressed, or pressured, I know that there is going to be a bad consequence. I know something bad is going to happen. I know when I am doing something good, because I feel happy, free from any problems. I think everybody could tell what is right and what is wrong, but most people don't express their opinions and simply look within themselves for the answer that is right or wrong.

In a situation where you know what is right and wrong, you know what you are supposed to do, but people do not always follow what they believe. I think everybody would know right from wrong if they balanced their emotions and feelings on the scale of right and wrong. Not everything you do is right or wrong, but everybody knows what is better for themselves physically and morally.

9TH GRADE

The difference between right and wrong is different every where you go. There are different expectations and rules that one must abide by. What you do at home or on the street with your friends cannot always be done in school. However, in a more general sense, there are set differences between right and wrong in my mind. Ever since I can remember I can recall being corrected, not scolded, but told that so and so is wrong and not to do that. I can also recall being praised for doing the right thing and not choosing to do wrong. If one doesn't learn the little differences when they are young, they will have trouble telling the difference when they are older. Knowing these differences is what keeps our society going. Without the differences our society would not be able to thrive. The differences are created by our society. What may be wrong here in New York City may not be wrong in China or Europe.

There is always a chance to do the right thing or to do the wrong thing. In some situations it could be hard to do the right thing and because of that the wrong thing tends to be chosen instead. I personally have not ever been put in a situation where the right thing was hard to do, but that does not necessarily mean that I always do the right thing. It just means that I don't have trouble doing it when I want to.

The differences between right and wrong are engraved in most children's heads from watching TV and going to school. The same differences are always restated: Say no to drugs, don't drink and drive, don't let your friends drink and drive. As one gets older, I know in this school you also learn to do the right without hesitation. Even in the little things, such as helping some one with their bags or helping someone study for a test. These areas are also right things. I find that what not to do is mentioned a lot more than what to do. This not only makes the right thing a wise choice but a scapegoat.

In our school at this time some people seem to be struggling to do the right thing. Things are being stolen and people end up having to beg for their stuff to be returned. This is a horrible thing and shows that not only our school but our society has failed in the same way when dealing with settling differences.

10TH GRADE

Society decides right from wrong. If one does not go by society's guidelines one is considered an outcast. In the 19th Century society considered it "right" to own a slave, but now it is considered "wrong" to own a slave. Today if someone owned a slave, he would be considered a "bad" person, an outcast.

I, like the other millions of people in the world, make my moral guidelines from what society says to do. Society uses its biggest propaganda machine, also known as the television, to get its guidelines out to the rest of the world. A good example of this is the drug commercials telling children not to use drugs because they are bad. This is what society believes, so the idea spreads through television.

My experience with this first came in the second grade. I was watching the TV and I saw my favorite cartoon hero telling me to wear a helmet when I ride my bike. When the weekend came and my friends and I went biking, I was sure to bring along my new "Teenage Mutant Ninja Turtle" bike helmet (the one that looked like a turtle shell). All my friends said it was corny to wear a helmet and they called me a geek, but I stood by what the turtles said. I wore that helmet with pride.

If that commercial had never aired and instead society told me not to wear a helmet, that wearing a helmet is dangerous, then I would have gone bareheaded that day, and so would all the children of America.

10TH GRADE

Would it be right for me to walk out of this room not finishing this essay? From my perspective I really could care less, but Mr. Morrison my adviser thinks it would be wrong.

I think that you are the person to judge whether something is right or wrong. And the society will judge your actions by what they think is right or wrong. In that way the society judges what is right and you obey them knowing that you will get punished if you do something that they think is wrong.

Getting back to where I started, the society, in this case the school, would not think of it as a good thing, but since there is no grade for this paper and there is no punishment, I'll chose wrong. See you!

11TH GRADE

Standing up for one's morals is always a very scary situation because morals differ from one person to another. So when I stand up for what I believe to be right, it doesn't necessarily mean that another individual shares my beliefs. This can cause major conflicts between individuals, groups of individuals, etc. This is why people tend to keep their opinions on what is right versus what is wrong a secret during situations which call on one's judgments. This is the easiest way to avoid confrontation, so this is the path most people, myself included, choose to take.

I believe that doing the right thing takes much more than courage, it takes a passionate heart and a willingness to be exposed to others' sometimes harsh opinions. When someone chooses to voice their opinions on ethics and morals, they are opening up a part of themselves that is quite vulnerable, a part of themselves that can only be justified by argument, not fact. But, one can take it to another level by acting on these beliefs. Those who do take action prove to be quite dangerous in the most extreme cases.

This occurred to my mother about a year ago. Seventh Avenue is always a busy place, where yuppies, lesbians, gays, and teenagers are constantly brushing by each other. On one crowded corner sat a woman who protested against women's pornography. She was parading around with explicit photography of the degrading ways in which women are portrayed in pornographic films, magazines, etc. My mother was walking around with her friend and her friend's child, who happened to be three at the time. His mother went over to the woman and said she believed that although her cause was a good one, it wasn't good for children to see pictures of naked women being forced into a meat grinder. This woman proceeded to call my mother's friend a "breeder" and numerous other curses. A few weeks later this same woman told another woman that she hoped that she was raped, so as to force some sense into her head.

This displays a warped sense of what is right. This woman believed that she was so right, no one else could be. Part of doing what's right and what's wrong has to do with one's willingness to listen to others and respect others' opinions. We would all be fighting constantly if we didn't accept others' opinions as their own, and agree to respect one another's ideas. If more people were able to agree to disagree, it would be much easier to get through life's tougher situations.

11TH GRADE

Truthfully, in my life I have, most likely, done more wrong than right, for it is by far much easier. Our teachers in life have taught us that to do the right thing takes courage and bravery and a good heart. They have tried their best to steer us away from wrong and ill will, without perhaps, realizing the impossibilities of such a task. They have tried to shape us: to mold us into perfect children who will grow up to be perfect adults, without perhaps, admitting to themselves that such a thing can never happen. For me, it is not a matter of right vs. wrong, good vs. bad. To me, the line between such poles is often thin or cloudy; sporadically fading in and out of distinction. I cannot recount a time when I have boldly stood in the face of wrong and told this evil temptress that she would not find a victim in me. I do not think it would be accurate of me to sit here and speak of my bravery in a difficult situation, for if there is one thing that my teachers in life have succeeded to teach me, it is not difference between right and wrong; it is that a person can only judge himself by his own standards. I have tried with much persistence to measure up to the expectations that have been laid out for me by those who care the most, but still I know that that is not the most important thing. Right and wrong are concepts, the boundaries of which I have not yet quite learned. I have tried to discover their truths and pretensions through my own struggles, and have, unfortunately, been only able to reach a rather inconclusive conclusion: that I still have not fully uncovered the true meaning of right. I have only uncovered a place within myself that knows what to do when perhaps I do not. Whether that is what is right, I do not feel I am entirely at liberty to say.

11TH GRADE

Once I was going to check if I had gotten an answer right. I was going to check with the person next to me, during the test. But this little voice inside my head said, "You should be doing this yourself, you cannot honestly prove your intelligence on someone else's. Don't be stupid, do the right thing." This little voice convinced me to do the "right" thing. But who was the author of this minute voice that had so much influence over my actions? My conscience.

In this all school write in, I don't think I can "ethically" say that I have ever used courage to decide what was right. I have only used my conscience. In my 15 years I have had a very sheltered life. I have never been faced with an ethical dilemma more than cheating on a test or taking an abandoned pencil off a desk when I know the owner. It has been very ethically challenging to write this piece without using conscience to tell me not to write a piece with no meaning.

I used my ethical courage not to blow this off as "another school write in" but to take it seriously and admit that I have no experience. I have decided to not make up some ethically courageous story of how I saved a kitten's life against my family's wishes, and to write an honest confession of how, because of my inexperience, I only have my conscience to guide me to do the right thing.

I feel that no matter how small or large the situation, it takes courage and conscience to get through it. Every situation is challenging in its own ethical way, but most often if you listen to yourself you can do what you feel is the ultimately right thing to do.

11TH GRADE

I know right from wrong because my parents taught me when I was very little. They imposed their good values and morals on me, making me a good, moral person. That is how I learned right from wrong.

There is no true definition for what is right and wrong. It all depends on the person; being a child that grew up in New York I was exposed to a lot of things that I believe to be wrong, such as stealing, littering and being simply mean and rude to other people. But because I had parents who enforced that these actions were wrong, I learned the difference between right and wrong.

In my eyes, a person who does the right thing and is moral is a person who is nice to others, helps others and doesn't do the things the society accepts as wrong. A person who does the wrong thing and is not moral is a person who does the things that society accepts as wrong. If a person doesn't know the difference between right and wrong then they are not a moral person.

11TH GRADE

The right thing to do is not always the easiest thing to do. As a society, we tend to gravitate towards the easy way to do things. This may not be the best way to accomplish goals, but who is to say what is right and wrong for an individual? In most cases, you learn some basic moral code from religion or parents, but a lot of people discount these ethics for different external reasons.

I am an ethical person even though I don't always stand up for what is right. Sometimes, I don't care enough to interfere and other times it takes more courage than I have to speak out. The times that I have not spoken up stick out in my mind more clearly than the times I have stood my ground. Once, as I rode the bus alone on a weekday evening, an older man and his extremely old mother got on the bus. Since there were only two others on the bus, I could hear every word he said to her. He talked about how much he hated "dirty Jews" and how stupid those "niggers" and "kikes" were. "That's why they always get beaten up," he said. This man went on and on about how dirty, stupid, and worthless Jews, blacks, Hispanics, and gays were.

Now, I am part Jewish, and even though I am not black, Hispanic, or gay, I was extremely offended, as were the other people on the bus. My first reaction was anger. I was so angry at this man, and felt pity for the poor mother who had to listen to her ignorant son in her last years of life. My anger quickly changed to superiority, for I realized how ignorant this man was. He was rambling on, sounding like a complete fool in a predominantly Jewish, black, Hispanic, gay area—Park Slope. He was speaking without thinking. Obviously he thought his ideas had some merit, or he wouldn't have spoken so loudly. But then, why did he and his mother look so unhappy? That day I did not say anything confrontational to the man, even though I sometimes regret it. But I look at it as more of a learning experience. Hatred breeds unhappiness, not power or happiness. So, in fact, that man may have felt in control, powerful, and better about himself by hating others, but in fact he was an ignorant, unhappy fool.

11TH GRADE

An ethical question is "What is right and what is wrong?" These questions pass through our mind every day, from adolescence to adulthood. As a child one has no comprehension of ethics, because they do not know better, but when one matures into an adult the range of questions and problems you will run into expands greatly. It is wrong if you're rich and you steal. But, if you're poverty stricken, is it wrong to steal food to survive? It is ethical not to steal, but if put in the situation where if you don't, your family will go hungry, whether something is right or wrong greatly depends on the situation and circumstances from which the problem has occurred. Your teachers say no fighting in school, yet, there are many countries at war now. My father always says to me and my sister when we're fighting that if you can't resolve the little problems in life, how can you expect to solve the big ones? Ethics all depends on the person. As for myself sitting in the cafeteria at Berkeley Carroll, I can think of a wide range of things that are right and wrong but, then I think of the many poverty stricken people here in the U.S. and all over the world, and my ethics change. It all depends. If I see a poor person steal food I would feel sympathy towards them, but if I see them steal the latest Nike sneakers I would probably feel disgust. Except that if I can afford to wear them why can't they, poor people are not bad people. Many people go by the saying "Let's spread the wealth," but a lot of those same people who complain that sports and movie stars make too much money don't think twice about not watching them.

11TH GRADE

The distinction between right and wrong is made early in your life and is usually influenced by your parents and your peers. Like all other ethical questions, people's views vary greatly. When I try to determine if something is right, I look at the situation. If what is proposed is harmful in some way to someone else, and I can recognize that at the time, then I consider it wrong and don't do it. But sometimes, people don't really look into something and figure out its effects on the people they care about, and when they see how it hurt someone close to them, their conscience makes them feel guilt, and that, to me, is the worst possible feeling.

You are taught as a young child that hitting and name-calling are wrong, and you either just accept that or do it anyway. But, in the end it is still evident that someone gets hurt, either physically or emotionally, by it. Later on through adolescence those ethical values you learned in kindergarten still hold true, but now they are more complex and harder to accept. It is much more difficult to say, "I'm not going to do this because it goes against my ethical beliefs," when everyone else seems very able to accept the wrong doings. People are afraid that if they don't drink and smoke or whatever, the cool kids won't like them. In my opinion, that's why so many ethical values are compromised by teenagers today.

My own personal experiences with this dilemma have been very scarce, considering how often it seems to happen to others. I think maybe it could be because I am a pretty good judge of character and my close friends are very much like me. This way, if I don't think something is right, they more than likely have the same view. Unlike my situation though, many children would do anything for attention and "to fit in." I can think of at least 4 or 5 close friends that I once had, that completely altered their character and personality and idea of self just to satisfy the "cool" people. It's upsetting to see what people are willing to do to be liked. And, in more cases than one, after that person has changed their personality and compromised their beliefs, that group of kids get sick of them and moves on, leaving behind someone with virtually no identity.

Your moral values and ethical beliefs make up a lot of who you are, and once you change them, you are no longer you. On the other side, if you are strongly grounded in your idea of ethics, you have strong character, which can overcome that need to be liked by everybody. You would never give in to the wrong thing, and if more people were like that, less talk would be needed about what it means to be ethical and how you know what is wrong from what is right.

12TH GRADE

If I were with a friend who stole something from someone else's backpack in the school, I know my immediate instinctual reaction would be to make sure this friend put it back.

The reason I know this would be doing "right"—there are basic codes or standards that everyone has to live by without putting up an argument. I'm talking about the value of respect that every individual must hold for him or herself and for others. Stealing defies the laws of respect. Without morals in a community, a friend cannot trust a friend.

Those who hold righteous codes and morals should take a leadership role and teach, enforce, and impose their beliefs on those who are disrespectful; and I mean disrespectful on any level—disrespect that makes the freshmen feel subordinate to the seniors and therefore prevents trust and unification of the school is the same level of disrespect in which the commons isn't left clean. I believe what's right is to create leadership in the students.

UPPER SCHOOL GRADE NOT AVAILABLE

I don't think that a school or a country can devise a set of morals and expect everyone to follow them voluntarily, or without question. Everyone has their own ideas of right and wrong. It is sometimes difficult for a person not to do something that they know is not right, and so they will go and do it anyway. I think that this is where opinions collide. What is right to you may be wrong to someone else.

If you do something like copying someone else's homework, and you think that it's okay but your teacher thinks that it is wrong, how would you resolve it? Chances are, you would get into trouble or something, and your teacher would have won. This is probably because there is a rule in your school against copying. If there wasn't one though, it wouldn't really be fair, because your teacher would win just because she has more authority than you, but not because what you did was wrong, and what she thinks is right.

I personally think it's wrong for our school to focus on what's right and wrong for as long as it has. No matter what we are told, or what our school wants us to believe, we have our own set of morals. We know for ourselves what's right and what's wrong, and we probably won't be persuaded to believe otherwise. I'm really not sure what this school hopes to gain in dealing so much with ethics. Obviously, there are basic principles that you should follow, but doesn't our school think we know that? We have been preached to our entire lives by our parents, teachers, baby sitters, and whoever else we have come in contact with. And now even though we are almost adults, we are still preached to.

To be honest, I can't recall a situation where I did the right thing, while others were doing the wrong things. That is because many of the things that I don't think are wrong are things that a lot of people do. But I don't really have a problem with this, unless other people's morals are imposed upon me. I don't want to be forced to do what they think is right, while I think it's wrong.

UPPER SCHOOL GRADE NOT AVAILABLE

When I was born, my parents flipped a coin to see which one of them would get to decide what is right while the other established what is wrong. My mother won. "Being right," she told me, "is largely a matter of explanation, while being 'Being in the right' is a matter of public opinion." She went on, "But, 'being righteous' can be neither explained nor swayed by public opinion. It is recognized universally." Being that I was still a newborn this was a bit much for me, so my mother gave me this example, "What if," she said, "you forget to hand in a paper one day but through talking with the teacher you make her believe that there were circumstances beyond your control. You then become right because you've explained away the wrongness of your action, and being that you're now right you become a member of the 'we are right committee' made up of people who have explained their way into being right, and who therefore get to decide how everyone else should act in order to be 'in the right.' But," she said, "despite all of your rightness you're still not righteous because although you're no longer wrong because you talked your way into being right, you still didn't do the essay, which was far from righteous and maybe even wrong, in spite of the fact that you've become right."

My dad's explanation was a lot simpler, "do what I say or else you're wrong." At least that I could understand.

APPENDIX B

Berkeley Carroll School Ethical Standards

This appendix contains the lists of ethical standards drawn up by each of the major constituencies of the Berkeley Carroll School as a sort of culminating activity to formally end our project. But in a way, these statements serve as a beginning and a way to continue our school's efforts to create, maintain, and enhance ethical awareness throughout our whole school community. We hope these lists will serve as examples for others to use to create their own standards through dialogue, openness, clarification, and cooperation. Then this book will have served its purpose.

Near the end of the school's three-year co-curricular study, it was decided that it would be important for each constituency of the school to have its own set of written ethical standards. In order to accomplish this task, each division director met with his/her student council to dialogue and discuss the creation of their ethical standards, and then presented their ideas to the entire division. Similarly, the Parent Association leaders and school administrators met to create their own sets of ethical standards. Each division's standards were hung in their classrooms and were also included in the divisional parent/student handbook.

We believe that the visual impact of seeing the ethical standards written out and hung on the classroom walls is a powerful way to promote ethical awareness and understanding in a school. The classroom teachers can often find ways to incorporate them into daily activities, including literary analysis, the study of history, the discussion of local and national issues, and, of course, solving student disputes.

Ethical Standards for Administrators
- Uphold the School's mission and model its values;
- Lead by example;
- Support the work of your colleagues;
- Respect each other's leadership and management styles;
- Exercise professional discretion;
- Respect and use appropriate decision-making channels;
- Be honest and fair;
- Listen to and respect individuals;
- Encourage diversity and maintain a community free of bias and harassment;
- Communicate expectations clearly; view feedback as a cooperative responsibility.

Ethical Standards for the Parents of the School
- Be familiar with and respect the mission, policies, and procedures of the school.
- Respect the decisions and policies of the school and communicate concerns directly to the appropriate school officials.
- Establish a partnership with faculty and administration to develop a strategy for your child's success.
- Support and participate in school activities, and encourage your child to do so as well.
- Respect and support the individuality and diversity of all members of the school community, including differences in teaching styles, parenting styles, and lifestyles.
- Model integrity and responsible behavior, while recognizing their effect on our children and on the larger community.
- Encourage and support the peaceful resolution of conflicts.
- Respect the privacy of other families and students in the school community.
- Communicate openly and honestly with other families in the school community regarding the health, safety, and well-being of our children.

Ethical Standards for Faculty
We, the faculty of the Berkeley Carroll School, model ethical behavior by:
- Upholding the School's mission statement;
- Respecting the individuality, diversity, and different learning styles of our students;
- Fostering responsibility and integrity in our students;
- Being aware of how our authority, words, and deeds affect our students;
- Guiding students towards peaceful resolution of conflicts;
- Being honest, fair, and consistent;

- Working with parents to create a strategy for their child's success;
- Exercising discretion in regard to students' privacy;
- Respecting the individuality, diversity, and different teaching styles and work of our colleagues;
- Communicating all types of information with faculty and administration through appropriate channels, and
- Representing our school and profession positively to the larger community.

Ethical Standards for Lower-School Students

- Treat other people the way you would like to be treated.
- Take good care of your surroundings.
- Be the best student you can be.
- Help the community and people who need help.
- Be kind. Be kind. Be kind.

Ethical Standards for Middle-School Students

- Treat other people the way you would like to be treated.
- Take responsibility for your behavior.
- Help to maintain a safe, non-violent environment in school.
- Help and encourage others when they need it.
- Respect school property and the property of others.
- Be open-minded.
- Be honest.

Ethical Standards for Upper-School Students

We, the students of Upper School, model ethical behavior to the best of our abilities by:

- Taking responsibility for and accepting the consequences of our actions;
- Helping to create a safe, non-violent environment;
- Taking an active role in creating the rules by which we abide;
- Placing individual responsibility before individuality;
- Neither judging nor discriminating against others based on their gender, race, religion, sexual orientation, age or personal appearance;
- Respecting the position of responsibility held by the faculty and administration;
- Leading by example;
- Being open-minded to new ideas;
- Following the Upper School Student–Parent Handbook;
- Helping and encouraging others in need;
- Respecting the ideas, feelings, beliefs, and privacy of all members of the community;
- Respecting the property of others and the physical plant of the school;
- Dealing with every issue in a fair and just manner.

Suggested Readings on Moral Theory and Ethics and Education

Aristotle. (2002). *Nicomachean ethics* (C. Rowe, Trans.). Oxford: Oxford University Press.

Becker, L., & Becker, C. (2001). *Encyclopedia of ethics* (2nd ed.). New York: Routledge.

Bellah, R., Madsen, R., Sullivan, W., Swidler, A., & Tipton, S. (1985). *Habits of the heart: Individualism and commitment in American life.* Berkeley: University of California Press.

Blackburn, S. (2002). *Being good: An introduction to ethics.* Oxford: Oxford University Press.

Bok, S. (1978). *Lying: Moral choice in public and private life.* New York: Vintage.

Broad, C. D. (1930). *Five types of ethical theory.* London: Routledge and Kegan Paul.

Bull, B., Fruehling, R., & Chattergy, V. (1992). *The ethics of multicultural and bilingual education.* New York: Teachers College Press.

Cahn, S., & Markie, P. (Eds.). (2002). *Ethics, history, theory and contemporary issues* (2nd ed.). New York: Oxford University Press.

Damon, W. (1988). *The moral child: Nurturing children's natural moral growth.* New York: The Free Press.

Edel, A. (2001). *Ethical theory and social change: The evolution of John Dewey's ethics.* New Brunswick, NJ: Transactia Publishers.

Gilligan, C. (1982). *In a different voice: Psychological theory and women's moral development.* Cambridge, MA: Harvard University Press.

Goldman, A. (2002). *Practical rules: When we need them and when we don't.* New York: Cambridge University Press.

Hansen, D. (2001). *Exploring the moral heart of teaching: Toward a teacher's creed.* New York: Teachers College Press.

Howe, K., & Miramontes, O. (1992). *The ethics of special education.* New York: Teachers College Press.

Kant, I. (1991). *The metaphysics of morals* (M. Gregor, Trans.). Cambridge, England: Cambridge University Press. (Original work published 1797).

Kohlberg, L. (1981). *The philosophy of moral development.* San Francisco: Harper & Row.

La Follette, H. (Ed.) (2000). *The Blackwell guide to ethical theory.* Malden, MA: Blackwell Publisher.

MacIntyre, A. (1984). *After virtue: A study in moral theory* (2nd ed.). Notre Dame, IN: University of Notre Dame Press.

Mill, J. S. (1957). *Utilitarianism* (O. Piest, Ed.). New York: Penguin. (Original work published in 1861).

Nash, R. (2002). *"Real world" ethics: Frameworks for education and human service professionals.* New York: Teachers College Press.

Nietzsche, F. (1989). *On the geneaology of morals* (W. Kaufmann, Trans.). New York: Vintage. (Original work published 1887)

Noddings, N. (1984). *Caring: A feminist approach to ethics and education.* Berkeley: University of California Press.

Noddings, N. (2002). *Educating moral people.* New York: Teachers College Press.

Oderberg, D. (2000). *Applied ethics: A non-consequentialist approach.* Malden, MA: Blackwell Publishers.

Rawls, J. (1971). *A theory of justice.* Cambridge, MA: Harvard University Press.

Simon, K. (2001). *Moral questions in the classroom: How to get kids to think deeply about real life and their school work.* New Haven, CT: Yale University Press.

Singer, P. (1993). *Practical ethics* (2nd ed.). Cambridge, England: Cambridge University Press.

Strike, K., Haller, E., & Soltis, J. (in press). *The ethics of school administration* (3rd ed.). New York: Teachers College Press.

Strike, K., & Soltis, J. (2004). *The ethics of teaching.* (4th ed.). New York: Teachers College Press.

White, P. (1996). *Civic virtues and public schools: Educating citizens for a democratic society.* New York: Teachers College Press.

Contributors
of Ethical Cases

Teacher/Student Cases
Sara Bennett
Beth Goldin
Linnet Jones
Marvin Pollock
Peter Shakeshaft
Daniel Tillman
Judith Valdez
Anonymous contributor

Teacher/Administrator Cases
Maxine Barnett
Patrick Bassett
Len Bloch
J. J. Cromer
Brigette de Wever
Kathleen Ellis
Linnet Jones
Henry Trevor
Anonymous contributors

Teacher/Parent(s) Cases
Shelly Adasko
Maggie Bendicksen
Alison Lankenau

Phyllis Lemkowitz
Hilary Greenfield Quist
Laurie Tyree
Anonymous contributors

Teacher/Teacher Cases
Denis Kohlmuller
Edward Martin
Jean Molot
Anonymous contributors

Parent(s)/Administrators Cases
Jon McGill
Wendy Schlemm
Dolores Toolan
Anonymous contributors

Heads/Trustees/School Cases
Reveta Bowers
Gardner P. Dunnan
Ann Mellow
Stewart Moss
Richard J. Soghoian
Christopher M. Teare
Bongsoon Zubay

***Student Understandings of
Right and Wrong***

LOWER SCHOOL:

Pre-K and Kindergarten
Fiona Adams
Rose Bagley
Kane Balser
Maxwell Coburn
Ethan Corcoran
Katherine Cunningham
Gregory Dorris
Jonathan Edelstein
Kelsey Eng
Erica Freeman
Eli Ginsburg
Benjamin Hirsch
Giancarlo Hirsch
Benjamin Kaltman
Oliver Kinkel
Bennett Kolber
Isabel McMullan
David Meister
Laura Mistretta
Julia Novack
Kathleen Rominger
Peter Rominger
Patrice Roth
Jonathan Skeete
Katharine Villios
Laura Wacker
Lily Zimmerman

Grades 1–4
Chloe Callahan Flintoft
Peter Damrosch
Colbert Lucey
Michael Patlingrao

MIDDLE AND UPPER SCHOOL:
Stuart Anderson
Emily Barrett
Jill Benson
Chantel Coleman
Ryan de Lorge
Kate Gately
Deborah Greig
Spike Gronim
Jessica Hochman
Karen Keltner
Nathalie Klein
Zoe Klein
Gillian Kotlen
Chloe Kroeter
Lauren McCabe
Aisha McCluer-Fakhari
Theresa Messina
David Mossberg
Will Murray
Monika Philips
Nicole Quinn
Nick Renzler
Omari Roberts
Anna Robertson
Bettina Schlegel
Dionne R. Sinckler
Kirsten Tempel
Stefan Vaubel
Julianne Zullo

About the Authors

After spending nearly thirty years in private schools, **Bongsoon Zubay**, Ed.D., entered the public education sector in 2002 as Director of the State University Urban Teacher Education Center (SUTEC) in New York City. In this role, she coordinated the urban student-teaching experiences of college seniors from sixteen four-year State University of New York (SUNY) campuses, and supported them during their stay through student teaching seminars. Bongsoon Zubay began her career as a teacher at the Dalton School in Manhattan and then spent twenty-five years as Head of the Berkeley Carroll School in Park Slope, Brooklyn. She believes that teaching, unlike other professions, can bring a high level of satisfaction, by allowing a person to both influence future generations and learn at the same time. She remains passionate about the critical importance of recruiting and retaining high-quality teachers in New York City public schools, and encouraged more SUNY graduates to teach in New York City urban schools so that they could bring out excellence in both their students and themselves.

Jonas F. Soltis is Teachers College, Columbia University's William Heard Kilpatrick Professor of Philosophy and Education Emeritus and past president of both the John Dewey Society and the Philosophy of Education Society. He was an early pioneer in the development of professional ethics case studies for educators and coauthor of *The Ethics of Teaching* and *The Ethics of School Administration*. He served as a consultant and seminar leader in many independent and public schools in the United States and Asia. He also served as a faculty member at the Klingenstein Summer Institute for Independent School Heads, and as a seminar leader for the Christian A. Johnson Foundation's Educational Leadership Program. Currently he is the series editor of Teachers College Press's Advances in Contemporary Educational Thought Series, and also series editor and coauthor of the Thinking About Education Series, now on its fourth editions, for pre- and in-service teachers.